JAMES ALBERIONE

JAMES ALBERIONE

"A marvel of this century"

THOUGHTS

St Paul Publications

FATHER JAMES ALBERIONE
A brief history of his life,
his times and his work

By Luigi Rolfo
Translated by Aloysius Milella

Title of the original Italian edition:
DON GIACOMO ALBERIONE: sempre proteso in avanti.
Published by Edizioni Paoline, 1982, following publication
in article form in "Il Cooperatore Paolino"

FATHER JAMES ALBERIONE: THOUGHTS
Fragments of apostolic spirituality
drawn from his writings and talks

Translated by Aloysius Milella

Title of the original Italian edition:
GIACOMO ALBERIONE: PENSIERI
Published by Edizioni Paoline, 1977

St Paul Publications
Middlegreen, Slough SL3 6BT, England

This edition: Copyright © St Paul Publications 1984
Published on April 4, 1984
to mark the centenary of the birth of James Alberione
Printed by the Society of St Paul, Slough
ISBN 085439 233 5

St Paul Publications is an activity of the priests and brothers
of the Society of St Paul and of the Daughters of St Paul who
promote the Christian message through the mass media

Contents

SECTION II: JAMES ALBERIONE

Thoughts:
fragments of apostolic spirituality
drawn from his writings and talks

Section I

JAMES ALBERIONE

"A marvel of this century"

A brief history
of his life, his times and his work

Preface

To write the life story of a man is always an arduous work. This is especially true when the subject embodies a variety of pointedly significant qualities. When writing then of a man of God, as the founder of the Pauline Family, Father James Alberione was, the arduousness becomes almost insuperable. For one is close to mystery.

Since his death on November 26th, 1971, five biographies have already appeared in the Italian language exploring the life of this exceptional priest, defined by Paul VI as "a marvel of this century" whose dream was to "make the Gospel penetrate to the core of the masses".

In this book, Father Luigi Rolfo, the author of a previous carefully documented biography of Alberione, reviews the highlights of his life in rapid sequence with clarity of style and deep filial love. It is an unhurried summing up of the 87 years of life of the Founder of ten Pauline institutes

Notwithstanding the conciseness of narration, it is easy to perceive the wealth of particulars that go beyond simple data and underline the image of the man, the priest, the founder, the apostle and prophet. He finds his just place in each of these categories.

From a reading of these pages, one understands that Father Alberione belongs to a class of men, moulded every now and then by the Lord, for a uniquely singular mission. In the same way, one grasps his dynamic of life and action, his "eagerly pressing forward" towards the totality of being the relentlessly pursued.

The Founder of the Pauline Family appears as a man firmly planted in history and among men. But the trajectory of his full life begins and ends in God, in whom he trusted with resolute confidence. "The Lord willed what was done; it was he who did everything".

G.D.C.

Origins

He was born at San Lorenzo di Fossano (Cuneo, Italy) on April 4th, 1884, the fifth son of Michael Alberione and Teresa Rose Allocco, modest farmers, natives of nearby Bra and therefore co-citizens of St Joseph Benedict Cottolengo. He was baptized the next day, named James after his godfather, a well-to-do uncle who was a very religious man. The same uncle proved a great help to James until he died tragically in 1916 and left him as co-heir of his estate.

The frail health of the baby, which had hastened his baptism, kept his mother in continuing anxiety. She never tired of recommending him to the *Madonna dei Fiori*, a Marian shrine in Bra. There she had brought and consecrated all of her baby sons, praying that the Lord would call one of them to his priesthood.

In November 1886, when James was not yet twenty months old, Michael Alberione moved his family to a farm house in Montecapriolo di Cherasco, where he hoped for better remuneration for all of his toil in the fields and those of his growing sons already at his side. Here, at the age of six, James began attending the local school three kilometres away, a distance that hardly frightened the peasants of that time, all proven walkers. Already in the course of this first year of school, James told his teacher, Rosina Cardona, and his companions that his ideal was to become a priest. He confirmed this each day with a great love of study, a conduct that set him apart from his classmates, and a spirit of piety that impressed his teachers and parish priest, Father G. B. Montersino. It was decided to admit him to First Communion at the age of eight-and-a-half years, something rare in those times. The general rule was to admit only children who had completed twelve years of age.

His brothers had interrupted their schooling in the early years of primary school to help in the work of the fields. Their father was a tall and big enough man though not very robust. James instead, was allowed to go through every stage of school up until first year of secondary school and always had good marks. Then, on the advice of his parish priest and with financial sacrifice on the part of his family, he was accepted into the minor seminary of Bra, then dependent on the Archdiocese of Turin. Here he spent three of the most serene years of his life, years of much study, reading, prayer, and even of very much praise and encouragement on the part of his superiors. They followed his precocious physical, mental and intellectual maturing with obvious pleasure.

He did not excel in intelligence. But he was known for his serious application to all the duties of his seminary life and an uncommon maturity. At an age when games are often a ruling passion, he devoted all of his free time to becoming better acquainted with the major problems of the Church and society, attuned to the conversations and instructions of adults. Given the short distance that separated his parents' home from the minor seminary, they could see him often and bring whatever they thought would be useful. During the summer holidays at home with the family, they left him free to spend the greater part of his time in prayer and reading, which he was never anxious to break off. Among his personal expenses, books and magazines were always at the top of the list.

The school year of 1899–1900 was as much a frenzy of activity for James as the three previous ones were calm and serene. At first, thanks to his wide reading on the subject, he became enthused with a missionary ideal. In accord with his friend and classmate, Pietro Valetti, he asked to be admitted to the Congregation of African Missionaries, founded in Algiers by Monsignor Lavigerie. But by the time a favourable reply to his request arrived from Africa, James had strangely lost every attraction for the missions. What had happened?

Perhaps a dubious book passed under the desk to him by a companion produced an upheaval in his simple and naive soul. Whatever it was, the change and disturbance was such that his seminary superiors decided to send him back to his family before the school year ended. No doubt, it was an error of inexperience, so easy in a sixteen-year-old who had never known anything outside the small farm world of his village and family. But it could also have been one of those "accidents" by which divine Providence served to orient the young seminarian towards the very special personal vocation to which he was being called. Who knows the inscrutable ways of God?

To Alba

In the quiet that returned after the brief storm, James sensed his aspiration for the priesthood more strongly than ever. Was it possible now for a young man to be accepted into another seminary after this recent dismal performance? The problem was not a small one. But his parish priest, Father Montersino was at his side helping him to solve it. He loved him like a son and had kept full confidence in him even when seeing him momentarily disoriented. With his prestige and refined diplomacy, he arranged for James to be admitted to the major seminary of Alba. In October 1900, he would begin studies in philosophy and theology. And in Alba, less than three months after his arrival at the seminary, during the night between December 31st, 1900, and January 1st, 1901, the Lord spoke to young Alberione. It happened in a way that is, and will always be, quite mysterious for us. But it was unmistakably clear to him.

James spent that night in Eucharistic adoration in the Cathedral of Alba. It overflowed with people who, following the directive of Pope Leo XIII, intended to consecrate the new century to Christ the Redeemer. And precisely during those hours of adoration, James had the profound conviction of being called by God to the awesome undertaking of challenging "the press with the press" so as to make the Gospel pierce through all the strata of society. As he wrote many years later, "He felt himself deeply obliged to prepare himself to do something for the Lord and for the men of the new century in which he would live".

Why the press? Because the years of Father Alberione's youth were years in which the press and journalism in particular, still very limited but in rapid expansion, aroused in many the taste of something new as a real moulder of public opinion. The saying had even been coined: "Whether it goes well or whether it goes bad, the world comes and goes as the newspapers decide". Everyone concurred that the press was "the king of the times", the most powerful among very powerful forces of the world, an omnipotent, telling tool. Whoever had the press in hand had the world in hand.

The Pope and Bishops heartily exhorted the faithful to avoid the "bad" press. At the same time, they were to strive hard to build up its counterpart, the good press. A well known German bishop had expressed his confidence in the efficacy of the press in this way: "If St Paul were alive today, he would be a journalist". And the first Catholic journalists, generally very polemical and aggressive, were as much the idols of the seminarians and young clergy as certain athletes of their day.

A fighter by temperament, James had, therefore, to consider it very natural that God had called him to serve the Church with the most effective means known to his time. Even if on a purely human plane he felt a compulsion to break away from mediocrity, he made up his mind to prepare himself for his future mission with all the ardour a sixteen-year-old was capable of.

His health had not improved with the passing of the years. The doctors who took care of him underscored the likelihood of premature death due to his chronic consumption as well as for the extremely austere regimen he had imposed upon himself. But he did not worry excessively about the doctors' judgement. He was so sure of one day accomplishing what God had asked of him that all human reasoning left him indifferent. He had abandoned himself without reserve into the hands of Providence, convinced that God had thought of everything—even of the health he would need.

An incomparable Guide

Entering the seminary of Alba, James discovered in his classmate, Agostino Borello, the one great friend of his life. He was a delicate lad, noble in thought and sentiment and already tried by physical and moral suffering. The two shared ideals, life goals and aspirations, spontaneously confiding each other's most intimate difficulties, certainly not wanting in those days. But a sickness considered incurable at the time brought Agostino to his grave within a year and a half. All that remained to the devastated James was the pained memory of innumerable solid examples, and they exacted a pledge at the tomb of his friend that they would never be forgotten.

In compensation, God put a priest at his side for the duration of his studies as a seminarian who was exceptional in virtue and learning, the Servant of God Francesco Chiesa. He was only twenty-six years old but already highly looked upon and admired throughout the diocese. He was James' philosophy professor, his confessor, spiritual director, and more, a sound model of genuine priestly life. Known by all of the seminarians as "the Theologian", Chiesa was also a convinced believer in the necessity of mobilizing the press for the service of the Gospel and actively lent his efforts to the first attempts at organizing it on a national scale.

Under his guidance, and in the light of the style of this incomparable teacher, now his closest confidant, young Alberione learned to give prayer the prime place among his duties. He learned to work with love under the gaze of God impervious to what others would say or do, and to profit from every spare moment of time to add to his increasing knowledge through study and carefully planned reading.

With growing confidence of being able to reach the priesthood without any thwarting impediment, the young seminarian re-examined and pondered the thoughts that had struck his mind the first night of the century. Like the seed mentioned in the Gospel, they were slowly defining themselves by natural evolution.

In practice, he already saw the glimmering outline of a potent organization of writers, editors, printers and distributors, men and women, all lay-persons, all animated by one purpose: making the

6 *An incomparable Guide*

Gospel and teachings of the Church known through a web of publications and reading material that would morally and materially sustain each other with every means. Never harbouring the slightest doubt of this mission of his, he threw himself into diligent preparation. He was attending to a full academic programme, but did his utmost to familiarize himself with the society he intended to challenge as a protagonist, especially broadening his knowledge of history.

It is significant that among the books he read during the period of advanced seminary studies and the first years of his priesthood, first place was given the voluminous texts of Civil and Church History of Cantù, Rohrbacher, and Hergenrother. He asserted that he read from them "twice a day for five years". Along with this preference for history, he found much pleasure in works of a liturgical character. The best authors who had written about the liturgy from the thirteenth century until then passed through his hands. He faithfully read the magazine, *Ephemerides Liturgicae*. For the special competence he quickly acquired in this material, and also for the inclination he demonstrated for liturgical functions, the Bishop of Alba chose him as his master of ceremonies.

Theological studies at the seminary of Alba comprised four years of dogmatic theology and sacred scripture and two years of moral theology. Clerics were admitted to the priesthood during the first year of moral theology and immediately after, still residing in the seminary, they were expected to exercise a pastoral ministry in the parishes of the city and its neighbouring towns.

Young Alberione was admitted to tonsure and minor orders on June 24th, 1906, soon after his twenty-second birthday. Five days later, he became a sub-deacon definitively committing himself to serving the Lord in the clerical state and permanently assuming the obligations of celibacy and the recitation of the breviary.

The hour of priesthood arrived for him on June 29th, 1907. He was ordained by his bishop, Giuseppe Francesco Re, along with ten classmates. The following day, June 30th, he celebrated his first Mass in the parish church of San Martino at Cherasco, the adopted town of his family. No doubt the happiest person among those present at this Mass was the mother of the newly ordained. The prayer she had ardently raised to God over so many years was fulfilled that day. God had taken one of her sons to himself.

At Narzole

Like all priests at the moment of entering the clerical state, Father Alberione had promised his bishop "respect and obedience". In the exercise of this obedience, he did not return to the seminary to complete his studies at the end of the summer of 1907 as regulations prescribed, but found himself instead assigned to pastoral ministry at Narzole, a town of some two thousand people. What he discovered here was a disabled parish priest unable to attend to any pastoral activity whatever, an unhappy assistant who promptly slammed the door and left, and another assistant of immense good will who was eventually named administrator of the parish of San Nazario in an outlying district of the same Narzole. The whole weight of the parish would then have fallen on the slight shoulders of Father Alberione had the bishop not sent him help in the precious person of a fellow townsman, Father Giovanni Bergui. He was a priest who had shown an outstanding capacity for preaching and catechizing the young from his earliest years.

The Narzole townsfolk were not slow in understanding that their diminutive thin assistant was an uncommon priest. They observed him in church, absorbed in prayer more often than the others. This helped dispose them to listen to him with greater respect. They were delighted with the new forms of charity he introduced from the first week of his ministry in favour of the most destitute people of the parish. They were grateful and took pleasure in noting that their boys looked for him often and loved to be in his company. Knowing that he was very poor, they could not but marvel at the discovery that he had personally taken it upon himself to maintain two boys of the parish at the diocesan seminary, one twelve years old, the other eleven, of extremely poor families.

The people also loved his sermons, always to the point and never excessively long. They liked his punctuality for every religious function. Father Alberione's combination of exquisitely priestly talents moved a few parishioners to attribute him with deeds they likened to the marvellous and extraordinary. But it is certain that the most objective and balanced among them limited their judgement to admiration and satisfaction that he was at their service.

The admiration of the townspeople of Narzole for his work was contagious. Even Father Giovanni Bergui agreed and having the chance to meet him and speak with Bishop Re, he privately told him: "Your Excellency, Father Alberione is being wasted in a parish like the one in Narzole. If there's a parish in the diocese that's in a very bad way, send him there. You will see it straightened out and put on its feet in quick time." Bishop Re was happy to hear such praise for a priest of whom he thought so highly. But he unhesitatingly let Father Bergui understand that he had no intention of accepting his suggestion. "I have in fact thought of Father Alberione for another office I consider of special importance. As you can see for yourself, I have this letter that I mean to mail to him. If you will do me the kindness of delivering it personally, I may know more quickly if he is disposed to accept it or not."

Spiritual Director of the seminary

Father Bergui returned to Narzole keenly anxious to know the content of the letter he carried. When Father Alberione revealed the bishop's proposal he was astonished. No less astonished was Father Alberione. After a first reading, he thought the letter had reached his hands by error, perhaps misaddressed. It was not possible that a bishop as wise as Bishop Re intended to entrust a fledgling young priest, not yet twenty-five years old, with the office of spiritual director of the clerics and seminarians of his seminary! By tradition, the office was always the charge of mature priests of long experience. Father Alberione made sure that this was truly the wish of his bishop. He reflected, consulted with his spiritual director and others of his teachers, finally deciding to accept when the elderly parish priest of Cherasco encouraged and exhorted him to hear the voice of God in his bishop.

So it was that after about fifteen months of priestly ordination, he was to go back to the seminary for an undetermined period, fully aware that he must apply himself to a work that was delicate as it was taxing. He would not shirk constant availability to the young men approaching him for direction and would dispose himself to hear the weekly confessions of the greater number of them. To make up for his lack of experience, he read, studied and reflected a lot, and travelled more than a few times to Turin to consult with the best known spiritual masters of that day.

Short of operating funds, the seminary of Alba searched for ways of easing expenses and reducing its staff. It wasn't long before Father Alberione found himself doubling as spiritual director and as its lecturing professor in Church history, sacred art and liturgy. The clerics who heard him in those first years especially remembered his lessons in history. His was a vision that was grandiose and totally original. He could not refuse invitations to preach in the parishes of the city and diocese. As the spiritual director of the seminary, he was now one of the best known priests of Alba's clergy. The prestige of his office and his good name bore weight when the parish priests needed help.

However, as much as numerous and sensitive commitments crammed his days, he could not but think ever more intensely about his personal vocation, convinced as he was that it had come directly from God during the first night of the century. In the ensuing years, he had come to believe that he could fulfill the will of God by being at the head of an organization of "writers, technicians and propagandists", men and women, who aimed at serving God by means of the press, then recognized as the most far-reaching instrument of its time. About 1910, however, as he himself says, his evolving reflections led him to a radical revision of his project. He understood himself called by God "to form an organization, *but religious*, where forces would be joined and education would be total, where doctrine would be more sound. A society of souls who would love God with their minds, strength, hearts, and offer their work for the Church content with a divine stipend".

Still all of this remained a deep stirring secretly locked within himself for a number of years. In a staid small city like Alba at the turn of the century, a poor and sickly priest of Father Alberione's experience was easily looked upon as an impractical dreamer when suddenly proposing to "form good and zealous propagandists to work for the press among groups in Catholic circles". This was what he told his Bishop when he asked his permission one day to buy a small print shop. Should he have evidenced a bent to lay the foundations of a new religious family, or indeed of a number of religious families as he harboured in his designs, he would have been treated as an irrational fanatic, even by most of the clergy. And this because in those very years, Pope St Pius X had written that there were an already excessive number of religious families and that it would be far better to aim at restricting their number rather than allow new foundations of Congregations for either men or women.

In the meantime, awaiting the hour of Providence, he began working unobtrusively for the realization of his projects. He had sent a twelve-year-old boy from Narzole to the seminary, Giuseppe Giaccardo by name, whom he saw as a possible future collaborator. At Benevello, a hilly area where he had gone a few times for his health, he had known another lad, Torquato Armani. He had directed him to the seminary at Bra with the intention of drawing him closer at the opportune moment. And in the same seminary of

Alba, where he could not but have hinted at times about his projects to the students and young priests, an enthusiasm had been aroused which was to bring abundant fruit many years later.

Very humble beginnings

Father Alberione used to say that the works of men resemble a pyramid: they have a broad base but narrow themselves increasingly. The works of God instead, resemble a kind of inverted pyramid: they begin with a point small base but enlarge their breadth more and more with the passage of time. If this be true, and recalling the circumstances of its birth, we must say that his was truly a work of God.

We are given precise and detailed information about its beginnings in a Report he made to his Ordinary, Bishop Re, February 16th, 1916.

A first step towards the great purpose of his life was the management of the diocesan news weekly, *Gazzetta d'Alba*. It had been put into his hands by the Diocesan Association of the Good Press on October 20th, 1913, and for which he was to receive an annual stipend of 200 Italian *Lire*. Four months later, on February 18th, 1914, he decided to buy the paper from the same Association, agreeing to absorb its standing debt of four thousand lire, a not inconsequential sum for those times.

On July 13th of that same year, he obtained permission from his bishop to acquire a small print shop not only for printing his paper but also for forming qualified typographers and distributors of the good press. The premises where he set up the printing operation in a building situated in Piazza Cherasca, now no longer existing, were lent to him by the owner. The money he needed to buy the print shop and other basic equipment came from selling his godfather's effects which he had received in inheritance after his death in February of that year.

The print shop of Father Alberione was very small. So was the weekly paper he owned. So too was the family by which he intended to catapult himself into the great field of the apostolate of the press. He had two boys with him. One was fifteen years old, the other thirteen. Neither had ever before seen a printing shop. For their apprenticeship in the printing crafts, he put them into the hands of a twenty-year-old hired hand whom he brought over from nearby Asti.

In this setting, on August 24th, 1914, the *Little Worker's Printing School* came into being. For brevity's sake, it was soon known simply as the Printing School, and it was to prove the embryo of the Society of St Paul and of the Pauline Family. The first crude job attempted by the two improvised typographers was the Catechism of Pius X. This was to testify to the rigorously religious character of the Printing School notwithstanding that its name suggested a worthy trade learning project like so many others ventured into by the clergy with the idea of giving dignified employment to youth left abandoned to themselves.

Father Alberione continued to reside in the seminary, a comparatively short distance from the print shop where his boys stayed. He retained his offices of spiritual director and professor, which involved him in at least four hours of teaching a day. He warmly welcomed the help offered to him a few weeks after the Printing School was launched in the person of Father Giuseppe Rosa of Asti, a former religious who agreed to stay with the boys throughout the day. But this promising arrangement was to last for a little under two years due to a conflict of views about the life preparation of the boys and the economic flimsiness of the situation.

The difficulties of the early years

As a result of sweeping changes that have invested every aspect of social life these last few decades, it is very difficult at a distance of some seventy years, to imagine the particular climate in which the Founder and his first boys lived during the first world war and the immediate subsequent years.

They did not have many friends. In the seminary where Father Alberione taught and held an important office, his project was followed with considerable diffidence. The rector openly said that he was a fool and was heading for resounding failure. Even the seminarians knew that they were to keep their distance from the boys of the Printing School if they were not to arouse suspicion in their superiors.

The bishop of the diocese, wise and prudent, kept a vigilant eye but let the undertaking go on. He wanted no part in opposing something perhaps willed by God. At the same time he was cautious in openly supporting a praiseworthy attempt which at times smacked of the reckless. The civil authorities had so many other serious problems to solve that they neither had the time nor the interest to worry themselves about an energetic idealist and his few boys. The townspeople looked on them with a certain curiosity when they would see them out together for an evening stroll. But few asked who they were or what they were about.

The one man who followed them more closely, caringly and admiringly than anyone else, and was ever ready for any sacrifice that would help them, was Canon Francesco Chiesa, the parish priest of the Church of Sts Cosmas and Damian. He saw them every morning at Mass in his church not far from the house of Father Alberione. He listened, counselled and encouraged with a disinterestedness and wisdom of which only men of God are capable.

The scarcity of means that the Founder had at his disposal, including premises of his own, forced him to roam and rent houses that were proportionate to the number of his boys. Since their number increased slowly if steadily, it was inevitable that they pick up their things and move to new quarters every year. To the disruption and disadvantage of the work and a considerable loss of time, even the printing plant had to be moved. With five hours of study and school each day, the first Paulines prepared themselves for the priesthood much like the diocesan seminarians. But another five hours given each day to typographical work, printing the diocesan newspaper, books and various parish bulletins, helped them earn what they needed to live.

It was a life of hardship and sacrifice that few of us today would find acceptable. They embraced it willingly both because they were accustomed to sacrifice from the time they were born and because the Founder fired them with enthusiasm at every opportunity, telling them of the great future of the apostolate of the press, a future he saw as already present.

In his sermons to his boys, in intructions, exhortations and in school, the Founder expounded the thoughts that had gripped his soul for many years and were the driving guides of his life. His conviction was contagious. The work he had begun was willed by God, who would sustain and defend it in spite of any contradiction, any difficulty created by the great war, even of any mistake he could make. The press, to which he had devoted himself without reserve, was the unquestionably urgent work for the Church and society and the noblest, most meritorious apostolate in which a man could spend his energies. "I am certain," he often told his boys, "that if God were to allow an Angel to freely come to this earth and earn merit, he would come here. . . . This is the place for doing good today".

As a consequence, both he and his boys were to have the overriding concern of not obstructing the work of God by sin or indolence. "Two things alone irk me," he would say, "that I am not yet sufficiently good and that you are not yet sufficiently holy. Only these two things trouble me, no others. The rest all comes of itself."

Those who observed Father Alberione and his work from the outside wondered how long he could keep things going on his own. His frail health was faltering and the difficulties of war were aggravating conditions in a country despairingly poor. Disheartened as he may have appeared to be, yet knowing that he had no intention of cutting short what had been started, indeed consolidating and expanding it every year, they no longer knew what to think of him. Even Father Alberione's mother, who had moved to Bra in 1910, came to know that many people had begun to consider him a wild scatter-brain. She went to her parish priest wondering and worrying about the attitude she should have in his regard. He knew Father Alberione very well and was an enthusiastic admirer. He reassured her. She should be at peace and consider it her special duty to thank God for having given her this son, and pray from her heart for him and his work.

A second family

Father Alberione's friends seriously worried about him. They were convinced that he could not possibly put together the money that was essential to the survival and realization of his work. But the question of money left him cold. "God," he told his own, "does not need money, only good young people."

He had taken the words of the Lord quite literally: "Seek first the kingdom of God and his justice, and the rest will be given in addition." Since he was utterly sure that he was truly seeking the the kingdom of God and striving to make it grow in the holiness of his own, he was also sure that the Lord, always faithful to his promises, would give him all "the rest" at the opportune moment, including money and including health, always so desperate.

Precisely for this unlimited confidence in Providence, the most remarkable characteristic of the earliest Pauline period, less than a year from the day on which he had gathered his first boys around him, he laid the foundation for a second religious family. He opened the *Workshop for Women* which, as he then communicated to his bishop, would have the purpose of "forming able and worthy catechists and teaching feminine oriented arts". At the same time, they would maintain "a small shop of books and religious articles, distribution being one of the goals of the Workshop, along with handling the retailing of what is not possible in the Printing School".

That Workshop was to be the initial cell of the Daughters of St Paul. According to the designs of Father Alberione, through door to door canvassing and the setting up of book centres, they were to distribute what Paulines were to write and publish. Canon Francesco Chiesa aided Father Alberione in this new venture by singling out Miss Angiolina Boffi as a possible first prospect for the Workshop. She was the most educated and energetic of the catechists in his parish.

Unable at first to dedicate themselves to other things, they provided for themselves by making uniforms for soldiers, a skill for which none of them was prepared and at which they did not always succeed. On Sundays and holidays they all taught catechism. Miss Boffi proved herself a true teacher in this and a strong animator of the group, perhaps excessively so.

In no time, however, they gravitated to the press. They organized a "lending library" with a few hundred books scraped up here and there. Then they opened a small book shop on the busiest street of the town. They also learned to handset part of the texts that Father Alebrione's boys were printing. In the printing plants of Alba and elsewhere, all type matter was composed by hand, a long, tedious and exacting process. Mechanical type-setting machines like the Linotype were as yet a privilege of the well established big city newspapers.

Ventures and proposals

A few years from the foundation of his undertaking, there were enough indications for Father Alberione to be convinced that a Religious Congregation consecrated entirely to the press was a highly felt priority in Catholic circles. In fact, even before the guns of the great war had stopped reverberating, Bishop Castelli of Susa in north Italy, had recourse to Father Alberione for advice and help in rescuing his floundering diocesan paper *Valsusa*. Whenever the press was at stake, he found it hard to back away. According to the terms of agreement reached with the bishop, he would send Misses Angiolina Boffi and Theresa Merlo (the future first Superior General of the Daughters of St Paul) to Susa to organize the work of publishing and diffusing the weekly, *Valsusa*. Other young girls were to go along to manage a small card and book shop.

The people of Susa grew in admiration of the modest, reserved girls who lived like religious even if they were not. And since they had no name as yet like other religious but professed a particular devotion to the Apostle St Paul, they began to be called, "Daughters of St Paul". Eventually this would become the official name of their Congregation. They remained in Susa until July 1922, when the Founder called all of them back to Alba to set them once and for all on the path of religious life according to the norms of Canon Law.

A rash of mindless strikes in the autumn of 1920, which inadvertently prepared the road for fascism, made it impossible to publish Turin's Catholic daily, *Il Momento*. Not seeing any other way out, the paper's directors turned to Father Alberione for help. As much as he was conscious of the huge difficulties besetting this enterprise and the risks he would be exposed to, Father Alberione decided to go to Turin personally. Taking his sturdiest lads with him, he left the younger ones behind in the care of Father Giuseppe Giaccardo, now the first Pauline priest.

The publication of a daily newspaper was an altogether different experience from anything they had ever come up against. But in spite of the pressure, they succeeded in getting a few issues out.

Widespread strikes in the mills then created such a drastic paper shortage that this gallant attempt was brought to a halt.

In the first half of the same year, 1920, Cardinal Pietro Maffi, Archbishop of Pisa, thought of entrusting Father Alberione with the technical management of the printing plant of the *Messaggero Toscano* and of various other weeklies. He was not thinking in terms of a brief period of emergency but of a minimum ten year arrangement. With great regret, and only for lack of personnel, Father Alberione turned down the Cardinal's offer. Not less than fifteen experienced typographers would have been required, which he did not have and whom he could not prepare in so short a time. It is not to be excluded that the Founder played with the idea on that occasion of shifting his entire undertaking to Pisa.

A more stable home

The first world war and an epidemic of "spanish flu" over (one of its victims was a candidate of the Daughters of St Paul), Father Alberione saw the pressing need for finally giving his twenty youths and many others asking to join them a more stable home. How? Buying a bigger house? Building one from the ground up? And where? In the city? On its outskirts?

By now a house was necessary. He had asked God for this for a long time, even adding this special petition to the usual morning and evening prayers of his youths: "O Lord, who said that we are more than sparrows, give us also our nest". Meanwhile he reflected, sought advice and kept his eyes open for a good opportunity.

A favourable possibility came towards the end of 1919. He believed that a six acre parcel of land on the outskirts of the city could very well fit into his plans. One Sunday he went to inspect the area, not far from the Alba–Alessandria rail line. The boys with him frolicked into their usual games while he scoured and studied the terrain. Gazing up and down, he paused, stared and had the strange impression of a house actually being built. It would become a reality before long, but that mysterious sensation made him think that the acquisition of this piece of land was meant in God's designs.

It was not to be an easy purchase. The land belonged to various owners and one of them, smelling a good deal, raised his price skyhigh. His wasn't only a love of money but the anti-clerical satisfaction of making things difficult for a priest. With patience, diplomacy and the help of an able and disinterested friend, Father Alberione was able to acquire all the land that seemed necessary to realize his plans. He set himself to building a large house on the corner nearest to the city.

He asked the municipal authorities of Cuneo for permission to build, and at the same time to be exempt from taxes because of the charitable character of his work. He went visiting the houses of a number of religious institutes to get ideas for what he would build. He met, talked and squabbled with architects insisting on the "beautiful but solid" construction he wanted at the lowest price. He reached the decision to put up a building that would measure ninety feet long, thirty-three feet wide and fifty-four feet high. It would be the tallest building yet seen in Alba and be built as soon as possible.

During the good weather season of 1921 the work of construction began. In one form or another, this was to practically go on without interruption for the next eight years. Faithful to the agreement reached, the builder turned over the finished ground floor of the building on June 15th, and completed the rest of the structure in the coming months. In this way, the now near forty Paulines could move into the first house of their own on August 10th. At the same time in Alba, preparations were going ahead for a diocesan Eucharistic Congress.

Right from the start, it was obvious that the house was too small. This happened in part because while it was being built, Father Alberione had acquired a large printing plant in Sesto San Giovanni (Milan) and had it transported to Alba. The printing presses occupied the entire space of the ground floor and the typesetting department was installed on the floor above. In such an expanded production situation it became indispensable to think of necessary storage area for paper and a stockroom for the books soon to pour out of the additional production equipment. So on December 21st, 1922, Father Alberione asked the municipality of Alba for the "authorization to extend the plant he had begun in the Malcotti region (in the territory of Alba) by another ninety feet. The construction is to be identical in dimension, space and light as the first edifice. *Excavations will begin immediately*".

The swiftness with which the building schemes of Father Alberione succeeded one another soon gave rise to the comment that he had been struck by a "brick-and-mortar sickness". In reality, far from being the victim of an illness or mania, he was forced to move out of pressing necessity. Indeed, thanks especially to the magazine *Vita Pastorale*, sent to all of Italy's parish priests, young candidates began flocking in not only from Alba, as they did in the early years, but from all over the Piedmont region and soon after from as far away as southern Italy. They arrived in such impressive numbers, if not always expected, that twenty enrolled Pauline students at the beginning of a school year would swell to as many as eighty by the time it ended!

Thus it was that by the autumn of 1922, the new building, erected in record time, was already overcrowded. Sensing the air of things, the bricklayers never earmarked the dismantled scaffolding for return to the construction yard but simply lined it up fifty yards away ready for re-mounting.

In fact, Father Alberione had already hurried the procedure for initiating construction again by the following spring. The new building would now no longer be ninety but one hundred and eighty feet in length, a twin copy of the one previously constructed but with a space separation of fifty feet to allow for the first phase of a grandiose church in honour of St Paul he now envisioned.

After what was noted about the great number of boys asking to be admitted, it should not be surprising that even the house built in 1923 quickly turned out to be insufficient. True, part of it was housing the Daughters of St Paul who were by now a growing religious family in their own right. Indeed in July 1922, nine of them had been admitted to religious profession. Heading the list was the youthful Theresa Merlo, chosen by Father Alberione to be the Superior General of the new born Congregation. "I elect her for twelve years," the Founder told them. "Afterwards, it's for you to decide."

Up to then, the Daughters of St Paul had been the extremely precious collaborators of the Founder and of the male community of Paulines, giving themselves to work in the kitchen, laundry and sewing. But growing rapidly in number, they too were looking hard for an independent house of their own. It would give them the chance to devote themselves as soon as possible to the specific apostolate for which they were born, that of marketplace diffusion of the Gospel.

The critical need of space, therefore, compelled Father Alberione to build a third house in 1924, similar in everything to the two already existing, but situated at an angle to the first so as to enclose a large courtyard where young aspirants could have their recreation and games. And before this was completed the contractor marked out the area where tons of earth would have to be moved to lay the foundations of the imposing church to be dedicated to St Paul.

By now even the church was a necessity. The chapel that had been built a short distance from the house was so small that the boys had to be divided into three groups each morning for Mass,

c

and the same for every other religious function. This involved a considerable loss of time and created a problem for regularity in study and work.

The hand of God

Like the townspeople of Alba at the time, readers can do no less than ask: how was it possible for this Father Alberione, so notoriously poor, and who to be more visibly so had given his wallet away as a diocesan priest, how was it possible for him to find the money needed to finance the building of houses and churches, buy machines and equipment, and assure the food and the lodgings of hundreds of boys who were incapable of earning their bread by the work of their hands?

The one plausible reply is that God does not ever delude those who totally trust in him and who work only for his glory. Through a thousand ways unknown to men, God allowed for the money that Father Alberione needed to reach him. And if it is true that not a few complaints were directed to Father Alberione for unpaid bills, it is also true, as he himself verified, that suppliers and creditors never lost faith in him. Not one of them ever lost, in his words, "a single penny".

There are a number of particulars about Father Alberione's life that are not comprehensible to us without allowing for the intervention of divine Providence. We cite a single example. The doctors who knew him were practically certain of his early death from chronic consumption. They had gone to the point of informing the Bishop of Alba that no cure could assure long life for him.

This illness, then so widespread and hardly ever curable, showed itself in him in a very grave form in 1923. It happened a few days after he had buried his mother and at a moment when he was intensely involved in the consolidation of his expanding enterprise. Three doctors were called for consultation and declared that in the most optimistic diagnosis possible he had eighteen months to live! Perfectly conscious of the state of his health and resigned to what seemed to be the dispositions of Providence, he readily arranged for his work to be carried on by his venerated teacher and guide, Francesco Chiesa. He had even requested and obtained approval for spending the brief time remaining to him in the Cottolengo Nursing Home of Alba.

As a house guest in the presbytery of Father Luigi Brovia,

the parish priest of Benevello (Cuneo) and a great admirer of his, he nursed his precarious condition almost exclusively on rest. It was as the doctors had prescribed: not even the recitation of the breviary nor the celebration of Mass were allowed. Slow recovery took place and in the first half of September he returned to Alba — not to enter the Cottolengo Nursing Home but to throw himself full-flight into a resumed round of intense and varied activity.

That Christmas, during the Midnight Mass he was celebrating in the chapel of the Sisters, his illness suddenly and violently overwhelmed him to the point that everyone feared his end was near. Astonishingly, he was to need only a few days of quiet recovery before plunging himself anew into every aspect of his bustling schedule. From that time and for the rest of the fifty years still ahead of him, nothing more was heard about consumption. Hundreds of persons were witnesses to this fact. None among them attempted an explanation.

A threefold Religious Family

The construction of houses and churches was an inevitable necessity Father Alberione had to accept along with all that came with it — the unending stream of persons coming and going, noise, trucks and materials, and interminable expenses. The ability of his bursar was not enough to eliminate or alleviate building debts. But this was not the principal anxiety weighing on Alberione. He had mainly to think of the ever growing number of persons living in these houses whom he meant to mould and organize into a threefold religious family.

The plan he had in mind from the first day of his activity as a founder did not in fact foresee the creation of three religious families at distinct intervals and with different ends. He had originally opted for a single entity ordered to the one scope of the apostolate of the press under a single Superior General. It was to have different areas of competence but they would be complementary: the *Society of St Paul*, the *Daughters of St Paul* and the *Sister Disciples of the Divine Master*.

What he perceived was a work of God dependent on grace, obtained through humble, habitual, constant and confident prayer. He therefore saw the family of Sister Disciples as a fundamental, essential element, called as they were to pray in silence and to the particular practice of uninterrupted Adoration of the Blessed Sacrament in Pauline chapels.

Sustained by this *laus perennis* (perennial praise) of God, besides of course their own personal prayer, Paulines would work for the spread of the Gospel and of Catholic thought through writing and publishing. And the Daughters of St Paul would take what was written and printed and channel it to readers through book centres and other forms of distribution, gearing themselves to reach people wherever they were.

The Founder was justly wary that Church authorities would not approve this innovative project of three religious families subject to a single Superior General. Unity of government, however, seemed so important to assure uniformity of doctrine and singleness of purpose that he felt it necessary to at least try to obtain its approval.

Meanwhile he briskly applied himself to giving his family a clearly defined form. There would be solid religious instruction based on the Word of God and the practice of three devotions: to Jesus the Divine Master, Way, Truth and Life, to the Apostle Paul, and to the Queen of the Apostles.

Devotion to St Paul had germinated in Father Alberione when he read his Letter to the Romans, so dense in doctrine and so rich in apostolic vigour. His confidence in the intercession of the Apostle was such that in 1953, reviewing what had been accomplished up to that moment, he wrote: "Everything is his. . . He moved and shed light on everything; he nurtured everything; he has been its guide, bursar, defender, support". Devotion to the Queen of the Apostles was based on the profound conviction that Our Lady was the inspiration of every new form of apostolate the Church needed. It had already been practiced by the seminarians in Alba. In 1922, Father Alberione gave heightened emphasis to this devotion when he asked the Dominican Sisters of Alba to paint a large image of her and prominently displayed it in the community chapel.

We must go back to 1900 to discover the origins of devotion to the Divine Master. At Christmas of that year, and for all of the following January, the rector of the seminary of Alba, Canon Vittorio Danusso, spoke to the seminarians of Jesus as Way, Truth and Life. Young Alberione sat among that group and always remembered this series of sermons. In his own time, he added the word "Master" (or Teacher) to Jesus and made the devotion more original and further consonant with the characteristics of the three religious families he founded. By this he meant to draw and consecrate the *whole man* to Christ. Christ is the Truth of the mind as a result of his teaching; he is the Way for the will by his example; and he is Life for the heart by his grace and, in particular, through the Eucharist. For this he often used these expressions: "the Eucharistic Divine Master", "the Divine Master in the tabernacle".

The arduous approval of the Society of St Paul

On November 23rd, 1921, Father Alberione consigned three documents to his Bishop. They were a brief history of the Society of St Paul, a draft of its Constitutions, and a letter requesting its approbation as a Congregation of diocesan right. The Bishop examined the documents attentively and had them studied by others. He wrote a personal letter to the Sacred Congregation of Religious and gave this to Father Alberione along with the duly examined documents. On January 2nd, 1922, Father Alberione was to personally present these to the Sacred Congregation in Rome and offer whatever explanation was required.

Two serious difficulties immediately surfaced in Rome. It was a rather unconventional innovation to propose a religious family given entirely to the spread of Christian thought through the press and not through the traditional means of preaching and the classroom. Besides, a religious family in publishing was exposed to the threat of growing wealthy and of making its style of life something of the comfortable middle class. The Sacred Congregation of Religious therefore advised the Bishop of Alba to let the new family continue to live "as a pious union of simple ecclesiastics and lay-persons" outside the framework of the religious life.

With a new letter dated November 16th, 1922, Bishop Re asked to be authorized to approve the Society of St Paul as a "Society of common life without public vows." After raising other difficulties, the reply of the Sacred Congregation of May 8th, 1923, authorized the Bishop to approve it as a "diocesan institute for men" whose members would be bound by simple promises rather than by vows. The situation was to remain as such for still a long time.

In the meantime, the work of Father Alberione grew remarkably and deepened its roots. Seeing this as evident proof of the blessing of God, the Founder appealed anew to the Sacred Congregation of Religious in May 1926. He asked straightforwardly for the approval of his undertaking as a Religious Congregation of Pontifical Right. This daring pretention would have probably gone nowhere were it not for the favourable intervention of Father Enrico Rosa, S.J., Editor of the prestigious *Civiltà Cattolica*. He spoke to Pius XI about Father Alberione and the apostolate of the press with such strong feeling that the Pope agreed to use his authority to help future difficulties be by-passed.

So it was that on July 30th, 1926, the Bishop of Alba was authorized to accede to Father Alberione's request. He asked him to revise the Constitutions prepared in 1923. Once Bishop Re was personally assured that they were "sufficiently clear and conformed to the Law", he erected the Society of St Paul as a "Clerical Congregation of Diocesan Right with public simple vows", and appointed Father James Alberione as its first Superior General. The date was March 12th, 1927.

The Daughters of St Paul

At the time of approving the Society of St Paul, Bishop Re warned Father Alberione that he would never move a finger to obtain similar approbation for the Daughters of St Paul. Evidently, he had not taken into account the tenacity and ingenuity by which our Founder knew how to achieve the goals fixed in his mind. Indeed on October 23rd of that same year, Bishop Re found himself persuaded to address a letter to the Sacred Congregation of Religious saying in effect that in the light of the experience of the preceding years, he judged it necessary to ask the authorization to raise the family of the Daughters of St Paul, already quite numerous, to a Congregation of Diocesan Right. The usual documents accompanied his letter.

No reply forthcoming, he sent a second letter on June 5th, 1928, and a third on August 1st of the same year. The questions raised by Rome were not a few. But a letter of Cardinal Laurenti dated December 12th, 1928, duly authorized Bishop Re to finally sign the decree canonically erecting the Congregation of the Daughters of St Paul. He did this on March 12th, 1929, appointing Theresa Merlo as its first Superior General, then directing her and her first four General Counsellors to pronounce their perpetual vows.

As for the Sister Disciples of the Divine Master, never mentioned in the correspondence with the Sacred Congregation of Religious, we read the following in the Constitutions of the Daughters of St Paul: "The Daughters of St Paul, a name extended also to the Sister Disciples, form a religious family alone, all professing the same religious life and subject to the same Constitutions, and enjoying the same privileges and spiritual favours".

Juridically speaking, therefore, they were (and were to be so for many years) an integral and indivisible part of the family of the Daughters of St Paul. In practice, however, they enjoyed an ample autonomy from the year 1922, developing their own scope as indicated by the Founder, following a particular pattern of life that distinguished them from the Daughters of St Paul even in dress. It was inevitable, therefore, that they would eventually arrive at forming a Congregation in themselves, a goal to be attained only on April 3rd, 1947.

Beginnings in Rome

During a visit to Rome in the Holy Year of 1925, a decision to open a house in the Eternal City had matured in Father Alberione. He later explained his reasons in a letter to his Bishop: to more conveniently accept aspirants from southern Italy; to more efficiently serve those parishes whose bulletins were being printed each month; to be near the teaching chair of truth. For this he had decided to appoint Father Giaccardo as head of the new community. His esteem for the Pope was commonly known.

Another reason why he was anxious to open a house in Rome was the importance of having a trusted representative at hand in caring for the interests of the Congregation before the official offices of the Holy See. In effect the presence of Father Giaccardo in Rome was to prove extremely advantageous during the drawn out study and procedures leading to the Society's approbation. This was not so much because of Giaccardo's particular ability as it was for his extraordinary goodness. He easily won the confidence of influential churchmen, as it happened with Cardinal Schuster, then the Abbot of the monastery of St Paul's Basilica outside the walls, of the curialist Bishop Pascucci, and of Father Enrico Rosa. This last had baffled his Jesuit confreres by openly referring to the Pauline priest as an extremely amiable saint!

Father Giaccardo arrived in Rome with fourteen teenage aspirants on January 15th and immediately opened a small printing operation with equipment sent from Alba. His toddling community would exercise its specific apostolate in this way and at the same time earn its daily bread. The early years of the new community were characterized by enduring sacrifices and great poverty. Yet an air of extreme serenity prevailed. Father Giaccardo was everything for that groping band of youngsters: superior, bursar, teacher, adviser, confessor, and more, a model of religious life. During that pioneering stage, his meagre talent for orgnization was more than supplanted by a truly exceptional goodness.

The Press Apostolate

For some years, Father Alberione cherished the idea of reviving a system of organization typical of the olden time Abbeys which in practice were compact self-sufficient states. Taking a page from their book and applying it to the now very developed house of Alba, he soon added rambling additions to its complex: a modest factory, furnace, small mill, oven, machine shop, carpentry shop, and shoemaking and tailoring to be done by the Sisters who were already overseeing all of the kitchen and laundry.

The results demonstrated, however, that this was an impracticable dream. The times were much too changed for this. His houses were not located in unvisited woods and forests as were the Abbeys of other eras, but in the hub of a modern society of specialized work. He had to reconsider then, more for practical reasons than lack of personnel, his idea of cultivating acres of poplar trees for one day fabricating all the paper he needed in his own mill.

Nonetheless, he tenaciously held to the ideal of exercising the apostolate of the press in its entirety "from the moment the written word was conceived up to the moment it became the printed word placed in the hands of readers". This ideal was integrally transmitted to his sons and daughters. He was ever convinced that this, and no other, was the mission of the Paulines, presenting it always as the indispensable condition for obtaining the blessing of God and achieving unerring results, even on a purely human scale. To be still clearer, he condensed his ideals into three words: write, print, diffuse.

To Write

In Father Alberione's scheme from the beginning, Pauline priests were to feel committed before God to make the Gospel known by means of the press, as diocesan priests were committed to make it known by means of preaching and the classroom. Naturally, the mission to write was globally entrusted to Pauline priests and not to each one individually, it hardly being conceivable that all would be endowed with the necessary capacity to write, or would find themselves in circumstances that would always make this a priority. But just as a Sister cook is co-responsible for the evangelizing mission of the missionaries she serves in her community, so those who do not write are co-reponsible and share in the Congregation's larger message-bearing mission.

In this mission of theirs, they must also try to enlist the aid of "Cooperators", priests, religious and lay-persons, disposed to gratuitously submit what they have written for a wider promotion of the Gospel. Father Alberione had the good fortune of finding an ideal and perhaps inimitable cooperator in the person of Canon Francesco Chiesa. He had been his inspiration and had written hundreds of articles for publication in all of the Pauline magazines. He provided manuscripts for dozens of books without ever asking a minimum of compensation, desiring only that what he wrote be spread and do some good.

As for the content and subject matter of Pauline writers, when Father Alberione was young he was inclined to make his approach a battling give-and-take defence of the Church and its teachings. But by the time he founded his religious family, he understood that it was far more beneficial to spread Christian thought in the simplest, clearest and most pastoral forms, leaving others to hassle over controversial issues, or be involved in head-on quarrels that were problematic, complex and of uncertain usefulness. "Free-for-all polemics are not for us," he repeated many times.

For many years, Father Alberione spoke exclusively of the press. At its peak, it was the recognized effective instrument by which the Church could be attacked or defended. But reading the signs of the times, he had already impressed upon the Paulines that in the exercise of their apostolate they were to opt for "the most rapid and far-reaching means". So when the motion picture, radio, records and television successively appeared, it naturally fell to him to adopt these promising and marvelous new instruments of social communication for the service of the Gospel. But without ever diminishing his enthusiasm for the press, which preserved its own inimitable efficacy.

To Print

The technical aspect of the apostolate was entrusted to the Disciples of the Divine Master, Pauline Brothers who live side by side with priests in every Pauline community and whom Father Alberione desired in greater numerical proportion. They were not to be excluded from writing or the creative aspects of the communications apostolate when they had the ability to make such a contribution. But heir main role was o take what the priests had written, examine it, weigh the audience to which it was best destined, and then put their technical know-how in motion. It was for them to transform a manuscript into a book or publication that would guarantee its widest acceptance, deciding the most suited format, typographical presentation and graphic expression.

At times, the Brothers' work would be mechanical, i.e., word-processing, photography, lithography, etc. At other times it would be organizational and managerial. More often it was to be highly aesthetic involving choices of type-face, method, illustration, etc. It became opportune and almost indispensable that at least some Brothers have specialized preparation and knowledge in art, graphics and design, and in the new technological systems of production in order to make a key contribution to the effectiveness of the printed visual and electronic word. It must be remembered that while the essential element of the apostolate of the press is the content of its message, the mode and form of its presentation is often decisive in its ultimate acceptance or rejection.

Press production would be an almost exclusive domain of the Brothers. Cooperators could be of assistance at times, but only rarely and nearly always indirectly.

To Promote

The direct and essential role in the all important process of bringing the finished book or publication to readers was given to the Daughters of St Paul. The Society of St Paul and the Daughters of St Paul are two independent Congregations, each with their own government and administration. But the Founder saw it as vital that they retain a unity and single-minded ideal in spreading the Gospel by means of the written, printed and audio-visual word. To assure this unity of purpose, as was noted, he would have disposed a single Superior General for both, had the laws of the Church permitted.

From 1929, the Daughters of St Paul exercised their specific apostolate in house-to-house promotion of books and reading material. Today, they exercise it through a chain of book centres, distribution agencies and other media-marketing forms located in every major city where they have a community. In the foreseeable future, it is not improbable that they will turn to Cooperators for help in managing those distribution focal points where broader coverage and effectiveness is hindered by a lack of adequate personnel.

The distinction of competences in the apostolate of the press is not so rigid as to preclude an inversion of roles. There are Daughters of St Paul and Brothers who write or create and prepare a variety of communications productions. There are priests who give themselves to areas of high technical coordination. And there are priests and Brothers as active in marketing and distribution as are the Daughters. Each one feels co-responsible for all of the apostolate and exercises it in the sector where circumstances or personal aptitude renders it most convenient.

Magazines and Periodicals originated by Father Alberione

To be active in the press apostolate to which they were consecrated and to allow for his religious to be creative in responding to their vocation, Father Alberione originated various periodicals over a span of twenty years. A good number of them have withstood the test of time. In their initial years of publication, these periodicals were all very modest. Not only for the awkward restrictions of the presses of that time or the inexperience of those who operated them, but also because it was the express will of the Founder that all Pauline periodicals aimed at a wide public should present themselves in the most readable and pastoral form.

First place among Pauline periodicals, not only in chronological order but also for originality in the way its production and delivery was then contrived belongs to *Vita Pastorale*. This monthly review for the clergy was founded in 1912 by Father Alberione. He was then the spiritual director of the seminary of Alba and without a penny to his name. He prepared the manuscripts by gleaning material from official documents and declarations of the Church, then sent them to a Turin based publisher (Marietti), who printed and mailed the magazine to a cross secion of Italian parish priests. His one condition to the publisher was that he be given free space to advertise the books of his own fledgling operation.

Having become a publisher himself, Father Alberione took the entire magazine operation to himself and from 1920 to 1930 made it the principal organ through which he made his religious family known in Italy. The magazine also served as a promotions springboard for everything published by the Paulines. In those years, many parish priests directed hopeful candidates to the Society of St Paul on the strength of what they read in *Vita Pastorale*. Today it is still sent to all of Italy's parish priests and considered a worthwhile pastoral aid.

To further promote and gain support for his work, the *Unione Cooperatori Buona Stampa* was issued for the first time in October 1918. With time, while holding to the editorial scope for

D

which it was founded, it enriched and expanded its content. From the time that the aim of the Society of St Paul was no longer expressed in the words "for the apostolate of the press", but rather in the broader formula "for the apostolate of publications", even this periodical underwent a revision of title: *Il Cooperatore Paolino*.

In September 1921, soon after the acquisition of the Sesto San Giovanni printing plant by Father Alberione and its installation in Alba, the first issue of *La Domenica* appeared. This was a weekly folder carrying the Gospel of the Sunday and short liturgical and ascetical reflections aimed at sanctifying the Lord's day. The format of this folder, copied extensively by Pauline foundations abroad, was altered after the liturgical reforms were introduced and made huge circulation gains in Italy. Each week it carries the entire readings of the Liturgy of the Word with explanatory notes. It is considered an invaluable parish aid not only for generating participation in the Eucharistic Celebration, but for many priests who are called to celebrate in the most improbable situations, where liturgical lectionaries are unavailable.

Una Buona Parola, another weekly folder begun in the year 1921, pointed at bringing its readers a word of truth and faith by commenting on the history of the Church and events of the day. It came out regularly until the difficult years of the last war. When peace returned, the folder was not revived but amalgamated to *La Domenica* which it closely resembled.

At Christmas 1924, an illustrated weekly for children saw its first issue, *Il Giornalino*. It quickly reached a circulation of 14,000 copies, remarkable for those days, and then in a short time more than doubled this figure. Today it bears enormous eye-appeal thanks to great strides in graphic and printing presentation.

Together with *Il Giornalino*, the Society of St Paul also published *L'Aspirante*, a bi-monthly for adolescents of the national Catholic Action organization. It was the one periodical not founded by Father Alberione but acquired from a zealous priest who had launched it but could no longer sustain it. For the wide appeal it enjoyed among young aspirants, the directors of the Catholic Action organization decided to re-acquire it in 1927 and handle its publication and circulation on their own.

An unrealized project

In February 1926, a month after his arrival in Rome, Father Giaccardo began the publication of a weekly called, *La Voce di Roma*. Its purpose was mainly to make the "words of the Pope" known, and it quickly produced special editions for the dioceses of Volterra, Rieti, Avezzano and Montefiascone. It sparked an idea in Father Alberione's mind for a project that was to prove too ambitious for his undermanned forces. He thought of setting up Pauline printing plants in reasonably quick time in the principal cities of every region in Italy to publish weekly newspapers for every diocese. He would count heavily on the cooperation of the local clergy for editorial matter and on the zeal of the Daughters of St Paul for distribution. He lacked the means, however, and the minimum of coordinating personnel. The project had to be abandoned after pilot attempts in the Marche and Calabria regions.

A magazine that was born with high hopes but soon spluttered in the face of numerous problems was *La Domenica Illustrata*. It set a ponderous editorial range for itself, until then untried by any other weekly magazine. Unsuccessful, it was relaunched under the logo *Focolare* but failed again. After the war, the magazine was given a fresh third start under the title, *Orizzonti*. But it never attracted the steady cultured audience it had to have and ceased publication in 1967.

A very interesting bi-monthly dealing with catechetics and apologetics began publication in 1933, *Dottrina e Fatti*. It became a monthly in 1936 and then ceased publication in 1939. After the war, the Daughters of St Paul revived it under the title, *Via, Verità e Vita* and made it a journal of thought. Naturally its circulation was limited but it drew high praise and consensus. Even the monthly magazine published by the Sister Disciples of the Divine Master, *La Vita in Cristo e nella* Chiesa is substantially a revised version of the *Bollettino Parrocchiale Liturgico* initiated by the Paulines in 1932 in support of the great liturgical movement then so widespread and which would prove a remote preparation for the coming liturgical reforms.

The one totally Marian publication begun by Father Alberione is *La Madre di Dio*. Only in recent years has it found its right format and readership absorbing a variety of other local Marian magazines and focusing its message more incisively. Its circulation is 100,000 copies.

Undoubtedly, the most known, developed and most fortunate of the magazines willed by Father Alberione is *Famiglia Cristiana*. It is also the most imitated by Paulines outside Italy. When it was founded over fifty years ago, it had eight pages and was entrusted to the Daughters of St Paul. It was meagerly illustrated, but thanks to the same Daughters going from door to door distributing each issue it built a circulation of 18,000 copies.

Passed into the hands of the Society of St Paul, it capitalized on new printing techniques, and especially after the war became a slick magazine product. With time, the initial eight pages multiplied to a hundred and sixty pages. The circulation leaped from 18,000 to a hundred times as much, outstripping every precedent for any existing Catholic periodical. It is so well known in Italy today that Paulines are often pointed out as the religious of *Famiglia Cristiana*.

Paulines abroad

At the beginning of 1926, Father Alberione opened a community of the Society of St Paul and Daughters of St Paul in Rome in order, as he put it, "to be closer to the Pope". It was also for having a trusted intimate like Father Giaccardo at hand to follow the practices necessary to obtain ecclesiastical permissions for the Institute from the Sacred Congregation of Religious. No other new foundation was then spoken of for five years.

Suddenly, in 1931, foundations outside Italy began following one another at a striking pace. At a half century's distance from this relevant historic date, recognition and admiration is due the first Paulines who docilely accepted the heavily demanding directives of the Founder with courage and an intrepid spirit of abnegation. He would send them to a country without knowledge of the language, without a penny, without prior agreement with the local Church authorities. Whatever their hardy good will, they were often to find themselves without the solace of a point of reference, personal acquaintance, or minimum of support. Waiting for their passports and visa documents, they begged money for their trips from friends and benefactors and would depart counting wholly on the assistance of Providence.

To Father Saverio Boano and Father Sebastiano Trosso (1893-1952), who reached Brazil on August 20th, 1931, Father Alberione sent a letter written from Genoa soon after seeing them sail. In it he marked out their programme and an outline of conduct valid for all future foundations:

"Your editions (publications)," he told them among other things, "are to be as pastoral as possible and keep to what St Paul would have done if he were alive today. Your spiritual and material way of doing things should be as pastoral as possible. Your distribution should be more pastoral still. Always and in everything imitate the house of Alba." To imitate the house of Alba meant to say that they should not only devote themselves to the press from the start, but be prepared to begin in the most absolute poverty and in the midst of any kind of difficulty.

Establishing himself at Sao Paulo in Brazil, Father Saverio

Boano decided to buy a religious-political weekly for Italian immigrants from the Capuchin Fathers called *La Squilla*. Around this weekly he organized a book publishing apostolate beginning with pastoral folders like *O Domingo*, an imitation of Alba's *La Domenica*. Father Boano did not remain in Brazil for long, returning to Italy in 1935 to regain his strength and health. But by then the Pauline Community he founded was well on its way and a number of young Brazilian aspirants had already inherited his enthusiasm.

After having remained a year in Brazil, Father Trosso left for Argentina. He established himself in Florida in the province of La Plata where he quickly began publishing parish bulletins and recruiting young candidates for the specific Pauline apostolate. He seemed a very robust man, but less than a year after arriving in Argentina his health failed and he had to be substituted by Father Torquato Armani (1899–1980). He returned to Italy for urgent medical attention.

Greater yet were the obstacles encountered by Father Francis Borrano finding acceptance in the United States. There, in 1932, a religious family dedicated to the press was looked on as an anomaly. Together with two later arriving confreres, he agreed to take on the responsibility of a parish in order to remain in the country, and only after long discussions and the gracious consideration of the Bishop of Youngstown, was he able to open a novitiate and begin preparing young men for the Pauline religious life.

Father Marcellino Gilli reached Paris on October 22nd, 1932, and set about distributing a few books he had imported from Italy. He worked to put up a small printing operation and with the best of good will founded a Pauline Community which was never destined to have great development. Much later, he was joined by Father Antonio Damonte whom the Founder had originally sent to Germany to open a foundation. He had returned to Italy discouraged after attempting in vain to establish Pauline bases in various cities of Germany and Belgium.

In Spain, Father Desiderio Costa arrived in Madrid in June 1934, transferring to Bilbao at the beginning of the following year. He succeeded in recruiting an affectionate group of enthusiastic boys despite the imminent danger of civil war. When the conflict broke out in 1936, he fled to France taking a few boys with him. The storm over, he returned to Bilbao and took up the interrupted pace of development with excellent results.

To the Far East

On November 9th, 1934, three Paulines, Father Paolo Marcellino (1920–1978), Father Lorenzo Bertero and Brother Michele Trappolini (1914–1978), set sail from the Adriatic port of Brindisi for Japan. On the same ship were two other confreres, Fathers Pius Bertino and Emilio Fassino who were still not sure whether their voyage would end in India or China. Only God knows how, but they eventually landed at Shanghai. They crossed the Yellow River and reached Hanchow where they were later joined by Father Giovanni Ghione (1893–1960), Father Ercole Canavero (1911–1975) and Brother Bernard Panaro (1920–1972). With this added able-bodied help, they finally chose to settle in Nanking and applied themselves to a very substantial editorial activity. Adversities were not wanting, chief among them their scant knowledge of the extremely difficult language.

In the autumn of 1934, Father Cesare Robaldo (1896–1977), Father Domenico Ravinna (1909–1982), ordained only a few months before, and Brother Valentino Brignone (1916–1955) arrived in Czestochowa, Poland. The following year, Fathers Bernard Borgogno and Marco Grossi left for the Philippines along with Brother Gregory Giuliodoro. At almost the same time, Father Michele Ambrosio (1902–1971), Father Guido Paganini and Brother Bernardino Ruffoli boarder a ship for India.

Hard times lie ahead for the young Pauline Communities of the Far East and Asia. All of the countries where foundations had been laid, China in particular, were to be thrown into the searing upheaval of either the Chinese-Japanese War or World War II. To the common hazards of bombardment, devastation, food shortages and changing governments, there was the added peril for many Paulines of finding themselves in countries at war with Italy and therefore subject to interrogation and the constant suspicion of subversive action.

Some were imprisoned in concentration camps; others were forced to move from one region to another. A few feared dying of hunger. But it was only the Pauline nucleus in China that was forced to abandon its adopted country. All the rest were able to remain and, once the war was over, to begin anew the broken efforts of consolidation. Not one Pauline suffered personal harm — a true blessing of Providence.

Pauline Sisters abroad

The directives of Father Alberione were very clear. When a community of Fathers and Brothers had given life to an editorial activity and then required a developing sector of distribution, it was time for the Daughters of St Paul to arrive and locate themselves at a near enough distance to work in close collaboration.

Everything did not always go well. Unforeseeable problems at times, or a certain impatience indicative of the determination of Father Alberione, did not allow for due preparation of their arrival. Their coming too soon often meant a scouring about on their own for books and materials to distribute. No less than their Pauline confreres, they too knew the sharp edges of beginning from zero. It is very indicative that the first two Sisters to arrive in Brazil on October 21st, 1931, a Daughter of St Paul and a Sister Disciple, had all to do to avoid being summarily sent back by the local Church authorities. They disguised themselves in civil dress and lived for two years as clandestine religious, working as housekeepers in the Pauline Community. But this imposed detainment gave them valuable time to learn about the country and its people, customs and language, essential for the fruitfulness of their future specific apostolate.

As for the Sister Disciples, whom the Founder always saw as the fundamental element of the apostolate for their prayer before the Tabernacle, they usually arrived when a Pauline Community was fairly well developed and a part of the house set aside for their residence.

Definitively to Rome

In July 1936, Father Alberione unexpectedly left the community of Alba, now nearly the size of a village, and transferred definitively to Rome. The house here was still quite limited, everyone living in a single building of average proportions. It was the confining restrictiveness of its work, under his eyes at every hour and turn, that kindled and stirred him to action.

He personally assumed the direction of every activity of the house, its printing plant and every work to be published. He returned to the classroom to teach theology, and intensified his preaching to the priests, the aspirants, the Daughters of St Paul, and the Sister Disciples, the silent and precious collaborators in every Pauline Community. He was to find his greatest consolation in the prompt generosity of the Sisters and their door to door distribution, an apostolic activity particularly dear to him.

A few months passed as he assessed the situation. Evaluating the prospects of the community at that stage, he decided to extend the house by sixty feet and at the same time renew the existing unaesthetic structure. Experience had taught him that new buildings would be filled soon enough with aspirants for the religious life and with new equipment for an expanded apostolate.

But the project closest to his heart at the time was the construction of a great church in honour of the Queen of the Apostles. It was to be situated at an equal distance from the houses of the Society and Daughters, and would be a place of worship suited to the solemn functions of the entire Pauline Family based in Rome. He had thought about the church for a long time. In 1933, he had asked an architect in Turin, Bartolomeo Gallo, the son of the architect who had designed the Church of St Paul in Alba, to draw up a model. Gallo was to travel to Rome at least five times to gather much needed information.

The church was spoken of very much, but for reasons unknown to everyone, the Founder postponed the project a number of times. A probable international war was being predicted by political analysts. This deterred him and made him hedge on its beginning. Preparations for construction were to be enormously complex involving the elimination of a small hill and the mounting of thousands of cubic feet of supportive concrete foundations. The expense would have been prohibitive and an extremely serious burden for the Congregation, already over its head in debt. Finally, however much praise was heaped on the projected model submitted by architect Gallo, Father Alberione did not care for it.

Meanwhile, the war that everyone feared broke out.

In honour of Jesus, the Good Shepherd

As far back as the early months of his priesthood, when he was assistant parish priest in Narzole, Father Alberione had thought of the possible founding of a religious family that would flank the action of priests in parish ministry. His then preoccupation with the press as the overriding scope of his life left this possibility stored away for the unknown future.

Now, thirty years later, he found himself returning with renewed interest to the idea of giving life to a religious family that would assist and, when needed, substitute the parish priest in the care of children, the catechetical instruction of the young and adults, visits to the sick, pastoral organization, and preparing the dying for eternity. It was a commendable and viable apostolate to be sure, but an exacting one. The slight possibility of life in community, an intense and many faceted external involvement, the necessity of spending considerable time in a variety of situations, and of dealing with different strata of persons, could tend to unanchored dispersion and become an impediment to the life of the spirit.

As he said then, however, these many reflections (and not a few sleepless nights) led him to the conclusion that the good that could be expected far outweighed the risks. Therefore, on the afternoon of October 7th, 1938, five Daughters of St Paul who knew they were to separate themselves from their Congregation for a particular mission to be entrusted to them by the Founder, went to live in an isolated small villa in Genzano, not far from the Appian Way, south of Rome. One of the Founder's brothers who was temporarily with him, accompanied the sisters to their new house to help them in the heavier work of their beginnings and to make them feel less insecure in their out-of-the-way isolation.

In short, these were the silent and poor circumstances in which the Congregation of the Sisters of the Good Shepherd, known familiarly as the *Pastorelle*, was born. If their nearest neighbours had little idea yet who they were, postulants began arriving in such numbers to the community that two other houses had to be hurriedly opened at Taranto and Perugia to receive them. But Italy had gone to war and for the first time Italians experienced the terror of bombardment. The house of the Pastorelle was exposed to too many dangers and had to be abandoned. The sisters dispersed and took temporary refuge in different parts of Italy.

When the armistice came, they returned together to their old house and started from scratch once more. They reorganized themselves with such surprising results that in the following year they opened a house in Brazil. Here their apostolate found a field as open as it was ripe. The Founder followed their development closely and intently, practically functioning as their one direct superior. It wasn't long before he found a valuable assistant in the person of Father Carlo Dragone, a gifted, wise, reflective Pauline, who was ever ready to carry out the directives of Father Alberione at whatever personal cost.

The Constitutions drawn up by the Founder in 1947 confirmed the Sisters' principal devotions as that of Jesus, the Good Shepherd; Mary, Mother of the Good Shepherd; and veneration of the Apostles Peter and Paul. A special article committed them to select "the rural centres and peripheries of large urban cities" and a "preferable field of apostolate". They were reminded in this to be like St Paul, debtors to all but in a particular way to the neediest and most insignificant of the great family of God. Only in January 1958, perhaps to avoid possible inconveniences from a too hasty emancipation, did the Founder give the Pastorelle a canonically erected government.

Another undertaking of Father Alberione was destined to honour Jesus the Good Shepherd during those years and proved perhaps the most taxing of his life. Contrary to the opinion of the great majority of his own, he wanted to launch a monthly review of pastoral theology to be called *Pastor Bonus*. It would be in Latin so as to be read by all the Bishops of the Church. He proposed to personally prepare the lead article of each issue touching on the duties of pastoral life, plus a meditation that would serve as a guide for a monthly retreat. The magazine was to be edited by Pauline priests but be open to the collaboration of all.

From November 1937, when its first issue was published, the magazine came out regularly until the tumultuous war made postal services impossible.

First steps in film-making

In August 1937, Father Alberione showed his first inclinations for putting the motion picture at the service of the Gospel. He charged a subdeacon, Father Gregorio Delpogetto, to familiarize himself as rapidly as he could with the world of films, studying, reading, observing, gathering information and consulting with experts in and beyond Italy. About a year later, an article appeared in the Vatican's *Osservatore Romano* telling about the missionary life of Cardinal Guglielmo Massaia and suggesting that it could prove a subject for a successful film. It was the incentive he needed for a decisive first step.

He unexpectedly summoned two priests of the house of Rome whom he knew to be favourable to an opening towards the film apostolate. He told them, "Let's go to St Paul's Basilica to pray for an important grace." In the basilica's Blessed Sacrament chapel he knelt on the pavement and remained absorbed in prayer for an hour. The two priests with him prayed as he did but they also kept a curious eye on him. A few days later, the grace for which they prayed became known when he announced, "The apostolate of the cinema can no longer be put off. Divine Providence will help us; let us not be afraid."

By disposition of the Founder, Father Delpogetto made contact with the author of the article published in the Vatican paper. He assured his co-operation as well as that of one of the Capuchin Fathers, who was happy to have the story of one of their outstanding missionary confreres made into a film. REF (Romana Editrice Films) was founded, a director and reputable cast of actors were assembled and placed under contract, and in a few months all was ready for the filming of *"Abuna Massaia"*, as Massaia had been called in his mission land of Abyssinia.

Many scenes were filmed on location in Abyssinia, then occupied by the Italian army. The other sequences were shot at the Cinecittà studios in Rome. The film earned an award at the Seventh Film Festival of Venice, especially commended for its photography and the sweeping breadth of many scenes. But it was also critized for the lack of emphasis given the missionary action of Massaia.

The criticism did not deter Father Alberione. He determined that REF would press ahead in its activity despite the paltry means it had at its disposal.

Light and comfort from the Tabernacle

Whoever speaks or writes about Father Alberione without having known him at close range, easily risks deforming him. If we were to line up the multiplicity and daring of his initiatives, the imposing array of houses and churches he built, his many relationships with the small and great of the world, his numerous trips to every continent, his preaching, his writing and his immense correspondence, we would have a hundred motives for seeing him as a man always on the move, a man always short of time, one unmindful of appointments, rarely available, a man with the same neurotic slant as so many of his contemporaries. But how far from reality such a misconception would take us!

Certainly, Father Alberione was a man of action by temperament and choice. He loved, admired and taught tenacious and methodical work. Unwilling to fall short of whatever he saw as his duty, he never allowed himself a holiday all his life. Not even in the full heat of the Roman summer did he accept to do his work in a cooler place. He always shrugged off games, hobbies and every kind of pastime. His overseas trips were never interrupted by incidental touring. He toiled incredibly much, indeed, but to use a favourite expression, he especially worked with his knees. There was no respite from work, but he prayed very, very much.

Profoundly convinced as a man and as a priest that he must work for the glory of God alone, but that he could achieve nothing without the light, strength and comfort that came from the Tabernacle, he unhesitatingly set aside whatever he was doing for prayer that was prescribed. He was never disposed to renounce prayer for any other work, however useful, urgent or noble it could be.

It was also a rule he gave his priests to consecrate no less than four hours a day to prayer, including the celebration of Mass and the recitation of the office. As Founder and superior, however, he felt himself obliged before God to do more than he counselled others to do. So throughout the peak period of his unsparing activity, from 1920 until his death, he spent a minimum of five hours a day in prayer before the Tabernacle. Three hours in the morning and two in the afternoon. Up before 4 each morning, he prepared to celebrate Mass. He prayed for himself and for all of his own still at rest, asking the Lord for the graces needed in the day just ahead.

But apart from this observable prayer which served as an example for all, those closeby noted that he prayed during the day's routine whenever unengaged in conversation, walking from one place to another, or when travelling by car, train or air. Not to mention the many hours during the day or in the heart of the night when he was forced to pace up and down in his office or room, waiting for the awful pain of his spinal deformation to ease, the same which forced him to stride crooked like, leaned to one side. This very heavy cross burdened him for more than twenty years. It forced him to leave his bed for hours nearly every night, to stop on long car trips, get out and amble about for relief, even to leave his seat on plane flights and attempt a few steps in the narrow aisle space. And it offered him the occasion to recite innumerable rosaries and other prayers.

Inalterable calm

Prayer and total abandonment to God, together cause and effect, produced an inalterable calm in Father Alberione in spite of an irascible temperament. Thanks to this he could face every problem, difficulty, surprise and contradiction that came from his position as the indisputable leader of various religious families. As might be expected, these were not always free of imbalanced, wincing, hostile or hasty members. Yet his steps, moves and reaction to developing situations were of a man who meant to get things done, but also of one who knew how to make time for everything. To be sure he would never be waited for, he always arrived on time for appointments and for the common acts of the community in which he found himself. If he found himself forced to wait, wherever he might be, nervous clock-watching was not his habit. If a chapel or church were close by, he would enter and pray until he was called.

He would go down to the reception parlour only when he thought it absolutely necessary. But every Pauline Father, Brother and Sister knew that they would be cordially received by him at whatever hours he was in his office. Whatever the reasons for seeing him, he listened with attention and without benevolently or impatiently rushing the person, even when he knew that others were waiting outside the door. When anyone was ready to leave, he invariably rose and took them to the door. Those who had not been received during office hours tried to catch him immediately after lunch or supper. Among the many who knocked at his office door, occasionally there were those who intended to insult or dress him down, even to threaten him. But always with little effect. Generally he did not argue, retort or become defensive but would pause for some moments and then without altering his tone of voice respond with a few words. We know of only one case where before a visitor's unpardonable coarseness he became livid with anger, rose, stalked to his adjacent bedroom and remained there for a few minutes to regain his composure. He came back to take up his conversation as though nothing had happened.

When he had free time, he worked on points for preaching, wrote articles, and more, attended to his vast correspondence. Up to his last day or until his sight permitted, he retained the admirable trait of replying to every letter he received as soon as possible, even to those casual cards sent him at Christmas and Easter. His replies were always brief and to the point, in an often telegraphic yet always complete style.

He would frequently ask his secretary to help him address his letters and stamp them. Due to the copious correspondence constantly arriving on his desk, the time he would have liked to give to reading and study was always very limited.

The tormenting days of the War

On May 10th, 1941, Pius XII signed the *decretum laudis*, a document by which the Holy See granted first stage approval to the Society of St Paul as a Religious Congregation of Pontifical Right.

Hitler had already unleashed the Second World War, predicting swift victory. The war dragged on instead and dangerously spread with no end in sight. On July 12th that year, when Father Alberione was received in private audience by the Pope to express his thanks for the Holy Father's benevolence towards the Congregation, Italy had entered the tragic conflict. Speaking with Father Alberione, the Pope told him of his delight to have approved an Institute dedicated to social communications, and warmly exhorted all Paulines to a sound interior life. But he could not hide his heavy anguish over the war, ranging unchecked in those days and spreading disastrously. He repeatedly begged Father Alberione and Father Giaccardo to "Pray! Pray also for the Pope! These suffering times make us feel the weight of our responsibilities."

When it was an impending evil everyone feared, Father Alberione did not speak very much of the war. He spoke even less of it when it exploded into a tremendous reality. He followed events in the newspapers for as long as that was possible, then turned to the radio for news reports. He did not fear the future of his work: he was deeply convinced that the works of God always emerge from terrible calamities reinforced. Therefore, more than the war, he thought of what he could do once it was over.

When the sirens sounded on the first night of the war in Italy, he did not join the rush to the basement shelter like the rest, but stopped at the doorway of the ground floor. He remained there like a silent, lonely watchman for the duration of the alarm. Certainly, in that moment, he was not only thinking of the hundred frightened persons crowded in the basement below but of all the Pauline Communities in Italy and abroad, a number of which had already suffered the hardships of war. And it is very probable that on that same night the idea came to his mind to confide the care of all his sons and daughters to the Queen of the Apostles, solemnly promising that if they would all be spared from harm, he would erect a great temple in her honour at this very place, over by the hill he could see from where he stood. From that moment, confidence in the protection of the Virgin became the topic to which he returned over and over again in conversation and correspondence with his own.

Did the faith of Father Alberione affect the course of events? We do not know. It is certain, however, that the Paulines were front-line participants in the trying drama of war, not a few of them deprived of everything they owned, exiled, imprisoned, detained in concentration camps. Yet not one of them was to suffer serious harm to his or her person. The fact cannot but be remarkable when one thinks only, for example, of the temerity of the Daughters of St Paul who continued to rove about Italy by every means even after all public transport had ceased to operate. It is true that luck helps the daring, but . . . it is easier to believe that faith generated their courage.

In thanksgiving to the Blessed Virgin

Measured as he always was in his judgements about possible divine interventions in human affairs, Father Alberione never outrightly declared that all Paulines had emerged unscathed from the horrors of war because of the special protection of the Virgin. But he was convinced of this. As Founder and guide of the Pauline Family, therefore, he felt obligated before God to keep his promise and to raise up a fitting temple in honour of the Queen of the Apostles. It would be situated at the geographic centre of the Pauline complex in Rome, for which not a few major problems had to be overcome.

First, he decided to terminate the services of Bartolomeo Gallo, the Turin architect who had drafted the first plan before the war, a plan he had found unsatisfactory. He invited the services of an architect living in Rome, Giuseppe Forneris, with whom he found it easier to discuss his ideas and reach an understanding. Despite the furious disappointment of Gallo and his threat to take legal action to have his agreement respected and indemnities paid, the Founder stood firm in his decision.

Determined as he was about this project, even before setting and pacifying this difficulty, he authorized the start of the truly colossal task of excavation. Nearly the entire massive area marked off as its construction site would have to be dug out to a depth of forty-two feet. They would have to go down a further forty-five feet to lay a sufficiet, bed-rock foundation on which to pour the hundreds of reinforced concrete pillars destined to hold up the whole edifice. And all of this was to be done with equipment that at best was simply rudimentary by builders' standards today.

Another major difficulty was the formidable cost of the project. Initial estimates were revised continuously because of the running devaluation of Italy's failing currency. The money worry aroused rampant scepticism among many Paulines for the project. But while supporters and the most stout-hearted were thinking twice, the question created no excessive anxiety for Father Alberione. From the first years of his life as a founder, he believed and taught that God did not need money for his works, only well-disposed hearts. And to demonstrate how much a marginal element money was in fact for him, he soon ordered building materials for a General House to be built a little more than three hundred feet from the site where the church was going up!

Up to then, he had governed the entire Congregation and was personally directing the Rome Pauline Community where he had resided since 1936. Given the development that his Institutes and work had now reached, it was indispensable that he be free to dedicate himself to the general problems of the Congregation and the Pauline Family. For this, he wanted an independent residence for himself and his immediate staff. The house he was building with great urgency would serve for this. Occupancy permits usually took time to be cleared, but before the bricklayers had left, the Paulines had their orders to begin moving in.

Father Alberione's confidence was not enough though to change the reality of things. The construction of the monumental temple, which in practice would contain three churches tiered one above the other, proved a bold, long and extremely costly enterprise. Its basic dimensions suggest why: its height was to be 243 feet, it would cover a surface of 8,649 square feet, a total volume of 109,574 cubic metres. Its artist, Giuseppe A. Santagata, worked for three years to cover the 3,600 sqare feet of the inner dome with distinct Marian frescoes.

It should amaze no one, therefore, that the Paulines besieged and begged the help of their Cooperators wherever they were, making these comments in their bulletins: "The new church of the Queen of the Apostles is our high task . . . The church is absorbing all of our energy and activity . . . Very much is being spent for the church . . . The difficulties are enormous . . .".

Father Alberione was relentless in following the work closely, more closely than he had done for any of his other undertakings. During his long journeys abroad in 1949 and 1952, he was kept minutely informed via letters and telegrams. Because of the church, he deferred or suspended many initiatives programmed for 1947 and the following years. He asked innumerable sacrifices of all the Pauline Family, but in particular way and with greater results from the Daughters of St Paul. They worked for at least five years in intensive promotion and exhautsing fund-raising for the church.

The essential stages of construction may be summarized as

follows. On August 19th, 1947, the Paulines of Rome assisted at the blessing and laying of the foundation stone by Cardinal Carlo Salotti. On December 23rd and 24th, 1951, the Fathers and Brothers, the Daughters of St Paul and Sister Disciples assembled together for the first time in the new crypt church for an hour of adoration, and on Christmas Eve they joined in the Solemn Mass of the Nativity. On August 20th, 1954, nine years from the start of its construction, Bishop Cunial blessed the upper church, the rightful Sanctuary of the Queen of the Apostles, and began a series of celebrations that culminated on the Feast of the Immaculate Conception.

On the evening of its consecration, Father Alberione said, or better, prayed before all his sons and daughters in these words during the Eucharistic adoration:

"From the conclusion of the war, knowing how much this church would cost in sacrifice, I chose its construction as a penance and reparation. It is you, O Mary, who saved us with a protection from Japan to France that suggested the miraculous. So, here today, a vow is fulfilled. We offer you this modest Sanctuary, the place of your throne as our Queen. Every brick represents the sacrifices of your sons and daughters and of many Cooperators whose names (even if they are unknown to men) are written in the register laid at your feet as a testimony of faith. Remember all of them, O Mary."

The first long journey

Father Alberione was so bound to his place and so unaccustomed to moving far, except for brief visits to the various houses in Italy, that at sixty years of age he still did not own a suitcase. For his first voyage overseas he borrowed one from a Sister.

In the autumn of 1945, he decided to visit the Pauline houses in the United States, Brazil and Argentina for the first time and see with his own eyes the many things that he could not be informed about during the war years. By now these communities were fourteen years old. He would be accompanied on this trip by the Superior General of the Daughters of St Paul, Mother Thecla Merlo, who would thus be able to visit the communities of her own Congregation. He also wanted the first Pauline who had reached the States, Father Borrano, to travel with them. He was an experienced ocean traveller and had a fine command of English. He had chosen to travel by sea not only for economic reasons but also to avoid appearing too distinct. In those days, religious who travelled by air were looked on disdainfully by their confreres, hardly respectful of the poverty they professed.

For that first voyage, however, even a sea-going vessel had to be judged an exaggerated luxury. Indeed, standing before the *Andrea Gritti* moored in the port of Naples that December 27th, 1945, he could be heard muttering: "And to think that as a boy I could ride a cart without being pulled by a horse or ox." This was the only fleeting reference to his childhood, because throughout the impending voyage he concentrated on gathering as much data and information about the countries in which he would soon find himself for the first time.

The rigorous schedule he fixed for visits to the houses, apart from the time he dedicated to prayer, was a whirl of endless appointments. Its like is not easily matched in the records of religious visitors. He calmly listened to each one who came to see him, just as he would in his office in Rome. But he preferred to speak and preach to the community, up to ten times a day, and nearly always on the obligations of religious life, apostolic zeal, the Last Things. With those who were responsible for the community and to whom he allowed ample freedom in adapting the general lines of the Institute, he examined projects, pored over its knottiest questions, suggested new initiatives especially for vocation recruitment and on a broad scale always aimed at imbuing confidence.

To the point of rudeness, he determinedly avoided meeting persons who asked to talk with him only out of vanity or curiosity. He was reluctant to meet the local Church authorities or groups of Italian immigrants. He accepted these with grace only when he understood that they were indispensable or useful to the life of the Pauline community. And, when he brought his programme to an end, the quickest means were to be at hand for getting him to the next community on his agenda.

Nevertheless, the voyage begun that December 27th was to conclude only by the end of the following March. For a man as jealous of his time and as conscious of pressing duties as Father Alberione, it was simply too much. So while going from one house to another across North and South America, he set every scruple aside : from then on he would travel only by air.

Expansion and consolidation

Even before the guns of war were stilled, Father Alberione sent Father Saverio Boano to open a house in Portugal. This was a time when crossing frontiers in Europe induced surveillance and unsettling suspicion. His journey was a zig-zag series of unscheduled stops, but he was able to find his way to Lisbon by October 13th, 1943. From the moment travel became less hazardous, the Founder sent Paulines in quick time to open new communities in Canada, Ireland, England, Mexico and Chile. Later there would be Africa, Colombia, Australia, Korea, Venezuela. It was harder to enter the countries of Latin America. But in those lands where foundations had already taken root, the ground was prepared for every form of the press apostolate. As in the past, all who were mission-bound were reminded by the Founder to dedicate themselves from the start to our specific apostolate. Now he also asked that international book centres be opened in the most important cities, that local language, culture and custom be studied in each country, and that the most suited locations be chosen as sites for our training centres. If they had the time and capacity, they were also to inform the central publishing office recently set up in the General House about the best books available for eventual translation.

From 1922 onwards, Father Alberione was impelled by an idea for which he would sacrifice all the gold in the world to see achieved. He was utterly convinced that it was God's will for the Sister Disciples of the Divine Master to be recognized as a religious congregation independent of the Daughters of St Paul. He had thought of them in this way from the beginning. Not to strain the good relationship he enjoyed with the Church authorities, he clenched his teeth and before the law accepted that they should figure as one family with the Daughters of St Paul, even if they enjoyed a large autonomy and were practically on their own.

Now on July 9th, 1945, at the suggestion of the Founder, the Superior General of the Daughters of St Paul requested the Sacred Congregation of Religious to sanction this autonomous distinction. No response came. On June 13th, 1946, a second request was made. This time, through its Secretary, Archbishop Pasetto, the Sacred Congregation replied coldly that the Sister Disciples were to remain Daughters of St Paul "once and for all" in name, habit, formation and the rest!

The explanation for such a surprisingly hard and biting refusal came to light months later. For reasons unknown, it was discovered that a trusted confidant had referred deliberately slanderous information regarding the Sister Disciples to Archbishop Pasetto. This had soured him and resulted in his rigid stance. The facts brought to light, it was not too difficult for Father Giaccardo, charged by the Founder to see the matter through in his name, to demonstrate that the Sacred Congregation had been terribly misinformed. Archbishop Pasetto, who at one time had been Apostolic Visitor to our community in Rome and had come to know and esteem Father Giaccardo, called him one day and in a startling turnabout said: "Father Alberione desires this; we will do it." On March 25th, 1947, the Sacred Congregation authorized the Bishop of Alba to canonically erect the new Institute. He did this by decree on Holy Thursday, April 3rd, 1947, a day liturgically dear to the Sister Disciples for its *par excellence* commemoration of the Eucharist and the Priesthood.

On January 12th, 1948, Pius XII granted the Congregation of the Sister Disciples the *decretum laudis* and the first approval of its Constitutions. That day, barely able to pronounce the words, Father Giaccardo celebrated his last Mass. He knew that the Pope was to perform this benevolent act towards the Sister Disciples and wanted to thank God with the remaining fibres of his energy. Brought to bed afterwards, which he would never again leave, he trepidly waited for the news of formal approval, the last great joy of his life.

This first Pauline priest, the devoted "lieutenant" of Father Alberione, the one whom all of the Pauline Family looked on as his eventual successor, died on the afternoon of January 24th, 1948, the feast of St Timothy, his namesake as a religious.

Timely detachment

At seventy years of age, Father Alberione preserved his freshness of mind intact, his method, punctuality to duty, his resistance to fatigue and his famous drive to "do and have done". He could not go on forever not feeling the passing of the years nor the subtraction of an inexhaustible physical energy. Surely the long season of furrowing and seeding had to give way to harvesting. From then, therefore, he took a series of steps that earmarked the stage of decisive and conclusive withdrawal.

On March 19th, 1954, he had distributed a booklet marking his seventieth birthday to all of his sons and daughters entitled: *To the Pauline Family*. It was the most careful and orderly of all the writings that had issued from his pen. In it, he exposed his definitive thought about vocation recruiting, human, religious and social formation, about work, Providence, and more in general, about the way to understand Pauline life.

For the fortieth anniversary of the Society of St Paul, occuring that same year, he submitted a manuscript to those editing the volume, *Mi Protendo in Avanti*, which was published also under the heading, *I Am With You*. For the first time here, he spoke of himself, recounting how the Lord had guided him to accomplish his will when and with what means he suggested. He wrote it at intervals when his work schedule allowed free moments. As a result, there is a choppiness to its logical and chronological order. It is, however, the one autobiographical document we possess and the only sure source for whomever wants an exact idea of Father Alberione's mission and work.

To assure the continuity of devotion to Jesus Master, Way, Truth and Life, the precious pearl of Pauline spirituality, he invited Father Carlo Dragone (perhaps the most gifted among his priests), to prepare an "Encyclopedia", a ponderous work meant to demonstrate how all the sciences could find their point of unity in Jesus Master. He likewise proposed that a Pauline Academy be founded with the name *Magisterium*. It would have as its official organ a magazine of the same title inviting the best writings of Pauline scholars and teachers. Unfortunately, the means he dis-

posed of were not equal to his plan and the results were far
inferior to his optimistic hopes.

Building a Retreat House in Ariccia (Rome), up to then among
the most sprawling and attractive of its kind, he intended to offer
all the members of the Pauline Family a common place of spiritual
renewal to which, according to his desires, all would return to
re-temper themselves at least once a year. For this, he willed that
each of the Pauline Institutes contribute to the building and
preparation of this house.

On April 4th, 1957, his seventy-third birthday, Father
Alberione opened the first General Chapter of the Congregation,
which he had put off for many years. The Chapter Delegates re-
confirmed him Superior General unanimously. He accepted and
in the presence of the representative of the Sacred Congregation
of Religious, declared that the time of paternal government had
ended. It would have been more convenient to have "a government altogether regular according to canon law".

In a certain way, the foundation of the *Sisters of the Queen
of the Apostles* was another concluding act of his life work. They
were joined to the other Pauline Institutes on June 29th, 1957,
when Father Alberione celebrated the 50th anniversary of his
priesthood. Their aim is to search out and guide young men and
women with signs of a vocation to the most suited Institutes of
their choice. In the mind of Father Alberione, they represented a
support and guarantee for the continuity of the religious families
he had founded before them.

"To complete the Pauline Family", as he himself said, Father
Alberione gave life to three Secular Institutes aggregated to the
Society of St Paul in the years 1958-59: *Jesus the Priest*, for
priests and bishops of the diocesan clergy; *St Gabriel the Archangel*, for young men, and *Our Lady of the Annunciation*, for
young women. He also expressed his yearning to found the
Institute of the Holy Family for married couples desirous of evangelical consecration in keeping with their state. But this was to
become a reality in November 1973, two years after his death.

A will surrendered

The esteem that Pope John XXIII nurtured for Father Alberione led him to place him among the Superior Generals called to be present at the Second Vatican Council. He was grateful to the Pope for this honour and was punctually present at every session. The lone contribution he offered the Council was that of prayer and example. He could not hear well and did not feel at home with the Latin spoken by the Council Fathers. He would never have thought of taking the floor before them and perhaps, as a man of action, he did not look too well on the multitude of their discussions. Few men worked as much and discussed as little as he.

For many years, he demanded all that his body could give and more. He imparted directives and guidance to four Religious Congregations and predisposed all of their varying activities. He listened to all who went to him for whatever reason, even if only to have his blessing before leaving on a new assignment. He was a tireless preacher in the Sanctuary of the Queen of the Apostles, at the Retreat House in Ariccia, and in the twelve Pauline Communities in Rome and its nearby environs. Every day he replied to dozens of letters. He wrote articles for the Pauline magazines and, nearly every year, undertook draining overseas journeys, exposing himself not only to excessive fatigue trying to save time, but to dangers to his life. Once, in Mexico, felled by the rarefied high altitude, he thought his hour had arrived. Another time in Japan, he was struck by an uncontrollable and extremely painful skin disease. It forced him to cut short his trip, undergo intense and debilitating treatment, and then be taken home on a stretcher once arrived at Rome's Airport.

It is true that his heart was exceptionally strong and that his methodical ways and remarkable self-possession permitted him to harness his energy to its best use. But time was soon to exact from him what it exacts from every mortal.

His spinal pains of many years became more throbbing and insistent. He was obliged to change his position very often during the night, breaking the rest he utterly needed. Only when he knelt in prayer did he remain immovable for hours at a time. It was as though he was then impervious to pain.

His eyesight and hearing progressively weakened, even if his faulty hearing could be concealed with discreet facility. He began to be slower and less secure in his writing, no longer always respecting the rules of syntax. Journeys took more and more out of him. At times, he would travel to Arricia to speak to a group of retreatants, but no sooner did he arrive that he would have to return home without getting out of the car. In time, even his tongue could not fluently pronounce every word. He would resort to a gesture to complete an unfinished phrase.

And so, one after the other, with unquestioned inner suffering, Father Alberione had to resign from the external occupations and duties that had crammed his life for over a half century. And this without a sign of peevishness, a word of disappointment.

In April 1969, when the Congregation held its Second General Chapter, the Founder followed the six-day schedule of its opening Spiritual Exercises scrupulously. But during the work of the Chapter, he would only be seen from time to time and on occasion but for a few fleeting moments.

Closer to God

In the same year of the Chapter, 1969, thanks to his strong heart, the Founder rather surprisingly overcame an attack of viral hepatitis. But in spite of being pronounced better by the doctors, what could he now do, 85-years-old and infirm? Suffer and pray. The possibility for speaking with people diminished, so he communicated at longer intervals with God. More and more he felt himself withdrawn from men, more and more closer to God in heart and thought. In view of the nearing encounter with him, he went to confession each evening as a kind of preparatory purification.

He continued to rise at 3.30 as he did when he was well. At 4, he would celebrate Mass on an altar set up in his adjacent office, and for which he prepared himself at length during the night hours of insomnia. After a small cup of coffee and a quick glance at the newspaper headlines, he would alternate between prayer and rest until 11 when his physician called. To the few who were admitted to see him before noon, or in the late afternoon, he liked to offer an image of the Queen of the Apostles with a written word of blessing when it was possible.

At lunch, always at 1 p.m., he enjoyed the company of the Brother and Sister nurse who were constantly attending him. He would recite the entire rosary with them, even if he had already recited one or more on his own. He loved to engage them in conversation after supper but was considerate of their needed rest. He was anxious to prolong the conversation as a way of somehow shortening the unending hours of his night. If he needed something during those hours, he would get up, open and close his door with great care not to disturb anyone, and find his way to a nearby table where a flask of coffee was always available. After coffee, he would take his cup, wash and dry it, return it to its place and silently make his way back to his room. At times, he would support himself on the altar where he would stop and pray at length, reflecting perhaps on the Mass he would celebrate the next day.

The condition of Father Alberione's health deteriorated with unexpected haste on November 22nd, 1971, with the symptons of a light bronchial infection. At midnigt on the 24th, the infection worsened seriously. In the early hours of the 25th, pneumonia set in. Father Luigi Zanoni, Father Alberione's successor as Superior General, gave him absolution and administered the Sacrament of the Sick. The last words heard from the lips of Father Alberione were: "I am praying for everyone."

On the morning of the 26th, Pope Paul VI, who had been kept informed of the Founder's condition, sent his personal blessing. That afternoon he decided to visit him in person. He arrived at the General House at 5 p.m. and was led to the Founder's room. Approaching his bedside, he called out in loud greeting, "Oh, Father Alberione, Father Alberione!" There was no response or recognition from the dying priest. The Pope knelt before him and prayed, concluding by imparting his absolution. Before leaving, he paused and gave a final apostolic blessing. Father Alberione died about an hour later. It was 6.25, the evening of November 26th, 1971. On this same day, sixty years before, his father passed away.

*   *   *

"He distributed more than twenty million copies of the Bible in the world", was the elegy most frequently repeated and which would have pleased him more than any other were he still among the living. For the rest, depending on the taste of whoever was writing about him, often without ever having known him, he was a saint, an apostle, a giant, a pioneer, a far-seeing priest, the founder of a paper empire!

For three days a stream of Pauline Fathers, Brothers, Sisters and Cooperators paid their respects and participated in the solemn concelebrations in the Sanctuary Church of the Queen of the Apostles.

His funeral took place in the circular crypt church of the Sanctuary on the 30th of November in the presence of six Cardinals, twenty Archbishops and Bishops, and officials of many Religious Orders and Congregations.

The remains of Father Alberione are laid in the lower crypt of the Sanctuary in a simple vault. The outer marble slab bears the inscription:

Father James Alberione
Founder and First Teacher
of the
Pauline Family
4 April 1884   26 November 1971

It has been said that the Sanctuary Church of the Queen of the Apostles, built by our Founder at immense sacrifice, will always "be *a concrete sign of the unity* of the Pauline Family in the variety of its Congregations". Now, in that same Sanctuary Church, the tomb of its common Founder, too, is a concrete sign of the unity to which the Paulines of the various Congregations and Institutes are drawn individually and collectively to pray, meditate and rediscover their faith, purpose and courage.

Section II

JAMES ALBERIONE

THOUGHTS

Fragments of apostolic spirituality
drawn from his writings and talks

Presentation

What is the human and spiritual stature of Father Alberione? What were the levers of his courage and action? What is there of himself and his thought to be usefully assimilated by the Christian of this dramatic age of history?

In various ways, these questions were posed to the religious family he founded. After his death, they began compiling and gathering together whatever Father Alberione had communicated by word and writing.

This series of extracts and excerpts will introduce the reader to his evangelical interiority and apostolic dynamism, the master-concepts of his spiritual thought and missionary action.

Father Alberione is rarely worried about style. His talks and writings are never elaborated on or refined. He does not search for originality of expression or doctrine. He insists on certain fundamentals, deeply etching his preferred concepts, re-proposing them over and over again. But we are struck by the ideas he brings out, especially in the field of his specific mission (the apostolate with the means of social communication, constructive and balanced poverty, religious life as a total response to God, prayer, etc.).

His audience was often young, unknowing and in need of formation and stimulus. This prompted him to use moderate but effective images taken from the activity itself. The thoughts themselves, without comment, are a treasure of spiritual teaching and one of the most precious fruits of his life.

G.R.

1

Conscious
of a mission

During fifty-five years, from August 20th, 1914, to August 6th, 1969, Father James Alberione founded and gave life to the Pauline Family (a group of ten institutions comprising religious congregations, secular institutes and a lay association). The Pauline Family was intended to respond to certain necessities of the Church in the twentieth century, especially to the urgency of promoting the Christian message through the means of social communication.

Recognizing the finger of God in these institutions, the hierarchical Church officially approved and launched this multi-faceted work.

Father Alberione was aware of being moved by God and of having been an instrument in his hands. He affirms this in humility and reveals certain stages of the actions of God in his life.

☐

☐ The hand of the Lord has been upon me from 1900 to 1960.[1] The will of the Lord is accomplished in spite of all that is lacking in this unworthy and inadequate instrument. From the start and throughout the journey, light, grace, inspiration, strength and vocations have come from the Tabernacle.

Every priest encounters two judgements: that of man and that of God. For the latter the only one that really counts, I beg everyone to obtain the mercy of the Lord for me in time. In the "to us sinners" of the Mass, we ask the mercy of being admitted into the company of the saints "not through our merits but through the richness of your pardon".

Before God and man, I feel the gravity of the mission entrusted to me by the Lord, who would have preferred a still more unworthy and incapable person — were there one. Nevertheless, for me and for everyone, this is the guarantee that the Lord has willed and done everything himself. Much like an artist who reaches for any brush of little worth and blind about the work to be executed, outlines inasmuch an appealing Divine Master, Jesus Christ.

We were founded on the Church and on the Vicar of Jesus Christ. This conviction inspires security, gladness and courage.

No matter what, Father Alberione is the instrument elected by God for his mission. Thus he has worked for God and according to the inspiration and will of God. For which everything has been approved by the highest authority on earth, and for which until now he has been followed by many generous souls. And for the future? Father Louis Colin replies: "When an institute with its rules has been approved, the superior or founder (unfortunate expression!) must be obeyed and must exact obedience".

1. In 1954, forty years after its foundation, a group of Pauline priests planned the first study of the Pauline Family and its Founder. The result was the commemorative volume published in Italian, *Mi Protendo in Avanti*. For that occasion, Father Alberione wrote down, in the third person, his most intimate recollections so that they would serve the above-mentioned study. He underlined the highlights and essential motivations by which God had guided him from his youth to the accomplishment of his mission. That precious manuscript was published in Italian under the title, *Abundantes divitiae gratiae suae*.

As an individual, instead, Father Joseph James will present himself for the judgement of God with the enormous responsibilities he faced in life.

It pleased the Lord to give me health and the possibility of completing the Pauline Family with the three secular institutes begun after the General Chapter of 1957. They are making headway.

Our life began in Jesus Christ and like Jesus Christ in the manger: "Glory to God in the highest, peace on earth to men of good will". I assure everyone that everything has been done only and always by the light of the Tabernacle and in obedience. The approval of the Church assures us that the institutions are valid and can lead to holiness, and that they conform to the needs of the times.

☐ The night which divided this century from the last was decisive for the specific mission and particular spirit in which the future apostolate was to be born and brought to full life.[1] Solemn and continuing adoration before Jesus exposed in the Blessed Sacrament was made in the Cathedral of Alba following midnight Mass. The seminarians in philosophy and theology were free to remain for as long as they wished.

A short time before, there had been a congress (the first he had assisted at). He had clearly understood the calm though profound and fascinating address given by Toniolo. He had read the plea of Leo XIII to pray for the century just beginning. Both spoke of the Church's necessities, of the new means of evil, of the duty of opposing the press, organization with organization, of making the Gospel penetrate the masses and bear upon social questions. . .

A particular light came from the host in greater understanding

---

1. The night between December 31st, 1900, and January 1st, 1901, when Alberione was sixteen years old, was decisive for his life and mission. He recalls it himself in the second passage of this chapter. In 1960, he conducted a thirty-day course of Spiritual Exercises for one hundred and twenty-five priests and brothers of the Society of St Paul, among whom were his first followers. He took the occasion to carefully explain, in definitive form, the meaning of the Constitutions and of the Pauline vocation, and to reconfirm before all of them the fundamental certainties which had supported his apostolic action.

of Jesus' invitation: "Come to me, all of you. . .". He seemed to understand the great Pope's heart, the invitation of the Church, and the true mission of the priesthood. What had been said by Toniolo about the duty of being apostles of today and of using the means exploited by adversaries also seemed clear. He felt a profound obligation to prepare to do something for the Lord, and for the men of the new century with whom he would live.

He had a sufficiently clear grasp of his own insignificance and at the same time an awareness of the words: "I am with you . . . until the end of the world", in the Eucharist. There was an awareness, too, that light, comfort and victory over evil could be obtained before Jesus in the host.

Looking into the future, he felt that other generous persons would share this urge to do something in the new century and that, organized together, the idea reiterated by Toniolo again and again could be realized: "Unite yourselves; finding you alone, the enemy will overcome you one by one".

Lasting for four hours after the Mass, he prayed: that the century would be born in the Eucharistic Christ; that new apostles would restore true meaning to law, school, literature, the press, public morality; that the Church would have a new missionary impulse; that the new means of apostolate would be used well; that society would welcome the great teachings of Leo XIII's encyclicals, especially those dealing with social questions and the liberty of the Church.

The Eucharist, the Gospel, the Pope, the new century, the new means, the doctrine of Count Paganuzzi regarding the Church, the necessity of new ranks of apostles — all of this became so fixed in his mind and heart as to dominate his every thought, prayer, interior work and aspiration from then on. An obligation was felt to serve the Church, the men of the new century and to work with others.

☐ At first he thought of a Catholic organization of writers, technicians, librarians, and Catholic booksellers, to whom he would give direction, work and a spirit of apostolate. . . But soon, in a time of greater enlightenment in 1910, he took a definitive step: there would be writers, technicians, distributors, but *religious men and women*.

On one hand, they would be brought to the highest perfection through the practice of the evangelical counsels joined to the merit of apostolic life. On the other hand, they would bring more unity, stability, continuity and a sense of the supernatural to the apostolate. An organization would be formed, but a religious one, where energies would be united, where dedication would be total, where doctrine would be more sound. And this society of souls, loving God with all their mind, strength and heart, would spend themselves in work for the Church, content with the divine stipend: "Receive a hundredfold, and possess life everlasting". He rejoiced, therefore, considering part of this army of souls as belonging to the Church on earth, and part as belonging to the Church in heaven.

☐ In a moment of particular difficulty, every aspect of conduct was re-examined to see if the action of grace had been personally impeded. It appeared that the Divine Master willed to reassure the Institute, now begun but a few years.

In a dream following on this, a response apparently came. In fact, Jesus Master said: "Do not be afraid, I am with you. From here I want to enlighten. Be sorry for your sins".

The 'from here' came from the Tabernacle, and was accentuated. It was to be understood that from him, the Master, would come all the light to be received.

He spoke to his spiritual director and gave an explanation of the particular details surrounding the figure of the Master. He replied: "Be at peace; dream or otherwise, what has been said is holy. Make it a practical programme of life and light for you and for all your members".

From then on, everything was directed to the Tabernacle and more and more derived from it.

☐ There were many who offered themselves in self-sacrifice for the success of the Institute. The Lord accepted the offering of some of these. . .

A circle of devout individuals who prayed in continuous adoration was formed. At the head of these was Canon Chiesa.

There were hardships of various kinds: personnel, finances,

written and verbal accusations. Day-to-day life was precarious and uncertain, but help always came from St Paul.

In meeting expenses, advice was sought and this examen made: Is this necessary? Is my intention right? Would we do this if we were at the point of death? If the answers were in the affirmative, trust was placed in God.

At times, necessities were grave and urgent, and all human resources and hope closed. Recourse was then made to prayer and an effort to do away with sin and every lack of poverty. Inconceivable solutions came, as well as money from unknown sources. Voluntary loans, new benefactors, other such things which could never be explained. The years and so many ominous forecasts of failure passed. The accusations of madness faded away, and everything took its course, under pressure perhaps, but in peace.

No creditor lost a penny, and suppliers, contractors and firms continued their confidence in us always. There were many benefactors whose charity bore triple fruit.

☐   As for this poor person, he has accomplished some part of the divine will but must disappear from the scene and from memory — even if, being the eldest, he gave to others what he had received from the Lord. It is as when the Mass is over: the priest takes off the chasuble and remains what he is before God.

I often pray: "Father, I am not worthy to be called your son; I have sinned against heaven and against you; keep me as your servant". It is in this way that I mean to be part of this admirable Pauline Family — as a servant, now and in heaven. There I will be concerned with those who use the most modern and efficacious means of doing good . . . in holiness, in Christ, and in the Church.

2

A dynamic vision
of man and of history

Training in hard work at home, a pledge at sixteen years of age to do something for the Lord and for men of the twentieth century, long meditations in his youth on world history (Cantu, Rohrbacher, Hergenrother), the mission which intensely committed his whole life to the creation of new energy for the service of the Church — all of this brought Father Alberione to a broad and dynamic vision of history. And through it he saw the life of man as an incessant, unchanging release of power for God and for mankind.

☐

☐ Life loses all sense when it excludes the doctrine of Providence. It becomes a blind process left to the mercy of physical forces and the malice of men. When faith in Providence is alive, however, the meaning of all human history is clearly defined. It is profound and elevating. It is God who conducts all things and makes converge, rather than the chance succession of intertwining individual passions and interests. Let history be well taught in the light of reason and faith.

Through faith in Providence we discover the God who cares for great and little things: from the atom, the hair on our heads, the lily of the field, to the development of the physical, intellectual and moral world. From its creation to its consummation, life is guided by the light of eternity, a universal judgement and the certainty of eternal justice.

How much reasoning is done without the use of reason, and without the light of the Gospel and the crucifix!

☐ In himself, man evidences and reproduces biblical history.

☐ Don't lose heart. Always preserve a healthy optimism. History is the teacher of life and our past experiences school us for the future. A battle lost, there is time for as long as we live to succeed in another.

"All things work together for good", when there is good will. For what turns out well, praise is given to God. For what turns out poorly, we humble ourselves and pray to do better. There is an excellent book called *The Art of Profiting from Our Faults*. The most terrible temptation is that of desperation, though the more common one is that of semi-desperation. Faith is the first virtue, but the second is hope. We honour and give homage to God by frequently affirming our belief in his goodness. A friend expressed bewilderment to Cantu wondering how he could have written so much and so well. The historian replied: "By perserverance".

☐   What does it mean to study? It means to commit oneself with industry. This attitude must accompany us until death. It should arouse everyone to want to learn new things. We cannot always do things in the same way during life. We have to progress each day, make improvement each day. After twenty years or more, we ought not to find ourselves at the same point. Nor can we say: "I am no longer a learner". All of us are obliged to learn!

☐   Discouragement is not permitted to the Christian. Much less the surrender of self to a world that lures humanity towards god-lessness. God is infinitely more powerful than man.

The Christian among men is the most decided advocate of scientific and technical progress. Only those who acknowledge themselves as sons of God are free of every slavery.

☐   He who does things makes mistakes (sometimes). But he who does nothing lives a continuous mistake.

☐   The only defeat in life is to yield to difficulties, to abandon the struggle. For man, to die fighting is to win. To desert the battlefield is to be conquered, and the situation of the vanquished is hell. "To the victor I will give hidden food." It is well worth the effort to fight for knowledge and for truth.

Man's unity must be rebuilt. A vocation does not consist of knowledge alone (not even an able exponent of theology, or an apologist, or a clever and fascinating writer constitutes such). A wall, like knowledge, however much a principal support, does not make for a house.

☐   The history of nations serves the greatest historical event: the Incarnation. By it God came to bring creatures to himself.

Young people, open your eyes to the general sweep of history, to the light of the Gospel, to the study of philosophy. For thousands of years, the fulness of time was prepared. Jesus Christ passed as the greatest figure of history, nay, as the God of history.

G

Now, through the Holy Spirit, he carries forward what he began. History, like our lives, flows into eternity.

Oriental and Greek history, Roman, medieval and modern history, general and world history — all are the immense work of the Father who creates and governs; of the Son who illumines and saves; of the Spirit who gives life and makes holy. Let Jesus Master always be your light in the study of the ages and of peoples.

Study history and declare that "to the immortal King of ages belongs honour and glory". Let the peoples of the east and west acknowledge Jesus Christ. May the Spirit go forth and renew the earth. Study history and learn from its achievement and mistakes. "And now, O leaders, understand; instruct yourselves, you who judge the earth."

☐   A healthy mind in a healthy body. God is life! Don't kill the body by whatever is excessive — play or work. Neither let your energies be diminished by imprudence or your values by neglect. Instead strive to develop these in yourself through proven educational methods. Develop your skills, improve the way you do your job, enlarge your sphere of action, your range of knowledge. For your own sake and those around you, develop your personality. Base it on truth and not on appearances. Work that is increased through one's industry is an imitation of God and brings us closer to him who is the purest of acts. This will also be a primary kind of mortification whether intellectual, moral or physical. "Imitate God as beloved children."

Money is a gift of God. Use it well. And if you can obtain more, multiply those undertakings that promote God's glory. "Put on your sandals", the angel said to Peter. He was even concerned about shoes! Take care of everything, your clothes, house furniture, books, means of work, etc.

Created things are meant to help us know God to bring us to love him and serve him worthily. Do not violate things, our nature, or our reason. Make use of everything as a means for glorifying God, for uplifting others, for achieving our purpose.

Practical examples can be found in the psalms and in the lives of the saints, especially in St Francis of Assisi, who even composed a hymn to the sun.

☐ It is not for us to talk about ourselves, though it can be useful at times. If I had worried myself about every little ailment of mine, I'd have been confined to my room for forty-five years now, closed off and avoiding draughts, asking to be served. Excessive care can weaken us. Without being imprudent, give the body as much exercise as it can take. When I am not pressed by time or necessity, I climb the stairs on foot, an exercise that is good for the health.

Let us not make an idol of ourselves.

☐ A man is educated when he has trained himself to use his freedom well.

☐ A period of reflection and examen, focusing judgement and prayer on ourselves, is such a beneficial thing. Any small exploration made with the idea of discovering ourselves brings us closer to the heights of self-knowledge. He who knows himself has indeed reached an important pinnacle. We can read a little of this book each day since it is always at our disposal. "That I may know myself" (St Augustine).

So much for arriving at human understandingg. But since we are of Jesus Christ, who is God, there must follow, "That I may know you". Jesus Christ is the transcendent graft on our nature and it is he who transforms our natural thought work and aspiration.

☐ If we bang our nose against a post in the dark, it's more than likely that we'll be more careful the next time around, since we have our nose at heart! Why is it that we don't do at least the same for our souls?

☐ Character examination is of great importance in relating to one's neighbour. A good character, knowing how to adapt to others, is a powerful lever for the apostolate. A faulty character is one of the serious obstacles to doing good. A person of character has strong convictions and strives with firmness and perseverance to conform his or her conduct accordingly. A good character is a blending of goodness and firmness, of gentleness and strength, of frankness and respect, winning the esteem and affection of those with whom it has to deal. A weak character instead, lacks frankness, goodness, finesse and firmness. By allowing selfishness to predominate, it becomes coarse and repugnant in manner, and at times even loathsome of its neighbour.

☐　Through faith, we recognize all men as companions in a journey towards eternity. Out of this rises the duty of mutual help.

☐　Through faith, we see all people as souls to whom we owe truth, edification and prayer.

3

Jesus Christ:
centre of thought and action

As an intimate follower of St Paul, Father Alberione had an altogether Christ-centred thought. The dynamic core of every one of its manifestations is found in the expression of the Apostle of the Gentiles: "I live no longer; it is Christ who lives in me" (Gal 2 : 20).

Reading the Gospel, he became enamoured of Christ the Master, the moulder of integral man. This inspired him to take the Divine Master as the point of reference of his spiritual life and the fountainhead of his apostolic mission. "You call me Master and you say well, for so I am" (Jn 13 : 13). "Go and make disciples of all nations" (Mt 29 : 29).

Under the inspiration of Leo XIII's encyclical aimed at guiding twentieth century man (*Tametsi futura*, November 1st, 1900), he learned to grasp the mystery and fulness of Christ in the trinomial of John (14 : 6): "I am the Way, the Truth and the Life". At the centre of all the thought, prayer and action of his religious family, Father Alberione therefore placed the Christ of these dynamic attributes, as revealed in the Gospel. "We were born to give man Jesus Christ, who is the Way, the Truth, and the Life."

☐

☐ Jesus Christ is the Master who best respected the human person, who develops our natural and supernatural faculties. He elevates and guides us to share in God's life in time and eternity.

☐ The Pauline Family aspires to live the Gospel of Jesus Christ, Way, Truth and Life, integrally, in the spirit of St Paul and under the watchful gaze of the Queen of the Apostles. It does not have many particular characteristics, special devotions, or excessive formalities. What is sought is life in Christ the Master and in the Church . . . The secret of greatness is to model ourselves on God, living in Christ.

Therefore, let it be ever clear: we are to live and work in the Church and for the Church. We are to insert ourselves like wild olives into the living olive, the Eucharistic Christ. We are to reflect on and be nourished by every phrase of the Gospel, in keeping with the spirit of St Paul . . . The whole man must find life in Jesus Christ, in a total love of God: one's intelligence, will, heart, physical strength — everything — one's nature, grace, and vocation for the apostolate. Ours is a vehicle that rests on and moves on four wheels: holiness, study, apostolate, poverty.

☐ "The common good requires that we have recourse to Jesus Christ, Way, Truth and Life" (Pope Leo XIII, Encyclical Letter, *Tametsi futura*).

The Pope says that genuine piety manifested during the Holy Year offers much promise for the new century. It is a piety directed to Jesus Christ, Way, Truth and Life.

The Pauline Family has accepted this as a sacred inheritance, knowing that receiving Jesus Christ according to the 'three principles necessary for salvation', is a matter of eternal life or loss for all. To receive him more fully means to be a Pauline: "There is salvation in no other. In fact, there does not exist under the heavens any other name given to men by which we can be saved".

If Jesus Christ alone is the fulness of salvation, it is necessary to find it in him alone. And the more we become part of him, the more we will live in spiritual health. Living Christ integrally, the whole man will be sound in mind, heart, will and body. There will be moral soundness. "We have been given a pledge of future glory."

☐ I don't have silver or gold, but I give you what I do have: Jesus Christ, the Way, Truth and Life.

☐ This Council (Vatican II) is the great, historical, religious fact of our time. It is Christianity's self-examination, a reflection on many points which can be reduced to three:

a) How much is Christian life practiced today in conformity with the Gospel? In what way is this life lived in the world today? In what is it lacking? What means are to be adopted for a valid purification and elevation in Jesus Christ, the Master? "Be perfect as your heavenly Father is perfect"; "Learn of me". *"I am the Way."*

b) How far has the doctrine of Jesus Christ been spread? With what acceptance and understanding? How has it been preserved in its wholeness and purity in the world? What are the means by which it can win all minds, mindful of the mandate of Jesus Christ, the Master, to the Church: "Teach all men"; "This is eternal life, that they may know the one, true God, and him alone whom he has sent, Jesus Christ". *"I am the Truth."*

c) How and in what way do we pray in Christ and in the Church "in spirit and in truth"? How and in what way are we fruitful in life and in grace as true sons of God as co-heirs of Jesus Christ? How can we better apply the words, "Our Father who art in heaven, hallowed be thy name. Thy kingdom come, thy will be done"? What are the difficulties and improvements in actual practice? "Prayer must be made without ceasing"; "Whatever you ask the Father in my name, it will be given you". *"I am the Life."*

☐ Let us make of ourselves the pen and tongue of God, through Jesus Christ, our Master.

☐   The process of sanctification is a process of Christ-ification: ". . . until Christ be formed in you". Therefore we will be holy in the measure in which we live the life of Jesus — or better, in the measure in which Jesus lives in us. "The Christian is another Christ." This is what St Paul says of himself: "I live, but no longer I; it is Christ who lives in me".

As the child gradually grows into the adult person, so it takes time until we reach "the virile age of Jesus Christ".

Jesus Christ is the Way, Truth and Life. Spiritual work involves: a) imitating the holiness of Jesus Christ who marks out the *way* by his example and teaching — "Be perfect"; b) a spirit of faith in Jesus Christ who is *Truth*, thinking according to the Gospel, the New Testament, and the Church which communicates them; c) grace, which is a participation in the *life* of Jesus Christ through the sacraments, and all the means of grace. This is how Jesus Christ, Way, Truth and Life, is formed in us: "Be conformed to him". So it is that Jesus Christ nourishes the soul in its faculties of will, intelligence [mind] and sentiment [heart].

☐   Christian, religious and priestly perfection lies in this: to establish ourselves totally in Jesus Master, Way (will), Truth (mind), and Life (sentiment) [heart]. Indeed this is the way to reach the supreme height of our personality: I who think in Jesus Christ, I who love in Jesus Christ, I who will in Jesus Christ. Or, Christ who thinks in me, who loves in me, who wills in me.

☐   To radically change our way of thinking, living and dying was the marvellous reversal desired and achieved by Jesus Christ. This is especially evident in the Beatitudes.

☐   When associated with the passion of Jesus Christ, every wearying effort becomes an element of individual and social redemption.

☐   Some are saying that what is needed today is another kind of education, another form of discipline, another style of living.

My reply: holiness is, and always consists in, living Jesus Christ as he is presented in the Gospel — the Way, Truth and Life. The mistake lies always in cutting ourselves off from the Gospel, from Jesus Christ, from the examples of the saints, from theology.

Religious life is always the one which Jesus taught, the one proposed by the Church, lived by religious who achieved sainthood and the one indicated by the Constitutions.

Conscientiousness is not rigorism. Laxity is not modernity but a worldliness of heart.

☐   The mystery of Christ the worker seems to me to be deeper than the mystery of the passion and death. So many years at the carpenter's bench! "Isn't this the carpenter's son?" "Isn't he the carpenter? The sweat on his forehead at Nazareth is no less redemptive than the sweat of blood in Gethsemane!

☐   The wearying labour of the apostolate is to be joined to the labour of Jesus.

The apostolate brings fatigue, discouragement, disappointment. There are those who fail to understand this. One wonders, have they understood the whole apostolate of Jesus? Let us think of him.

☐   A good part of the today's world suffers from a shortage of bread. There is a far greater shortage of the spiritual bread brought by Jesus Christ: "I am the bread of life". Countless people live completely unaware of their destiny. They have no other thought but the present. Yet in a comparatively short time, death will bring them to eternity. There are few to give them this bread. "There is no one to break it for them." They die of hunger without truly understanding their hunger. Jesus Christ is Bread-Truth. The apostle of the media of communication is another Jesus Christ who repeats to men of every age and place what Jesus Christ preached in his temporal life.

☐   It sometimes happens in books and sermons that little stress is given the preponderant role of Christ in our sanctification. Devotion to our Lord is presented as simply one of many means towards this end.

Our devotion and incorporation in Christ is the beginning and the end, the very substance itself of our supernatural life. Herein lies asceticism and mysticism. Practices are aids or consequences. With a genuine desire to make ourselves holy, we will avoid disputes and controversies about different schools of spirituality and instead commit ourselves to living the life of Christ more and more completely. This is how sanctity is unerringly reached. Do not deform the piety of the faithful nor promote ideas that confuse development.

Christological teaching on spiritual life may be summed up in the fundamental idea: live Christ as he defined himself, "I am the Way, the Truth and the Life".

☐   The work wrought by missionaries of religion and civilization is very much worthy of the enthusiasm and admiration of young people, the faithful, and every reasonable person. Theirs is a conquest of the world by truth and love, giving Jesus Christ to men and men to Jesus Christ.

4

The presence of the Mother of God

Founder of an apostolic family, Father Alberione was especially sensitive to the presence of the Mother of God in the realm of his apostolic labours, and invited his Congregation to venerate her under the title of *Queen of the Apostles*. The principal houses of these Congregations in Rome are located around the shrine-church he erected and dedicated to the Queen of the Apostles. It was his filial homage to the patroness of his entire work.

Every Marian title is simply the starting point of a deeper grasp of the whole reality of the Virgin Mary, in the mystery of Christ her Son. Father Alberione's perception of the Virgin Mother begins with his profound consideration of her as the Queen of the Apostles, bearer of the whole Christ and therefore the unsurpassed example of 'apostolate'.

☐

☐ There is nothing more valuable to be given this poor, proud world than Jesus Christ. Mary gave the world grace in Jesus Christ and continues to make this offering for all time. She is the universal mediatrix of grace and in this role is our mother. The world had need of Jesus Christ, Way, Truth and Life. Mary gives him now through apostles and apostolates which she inspires, forms, assists and crowns in fruitfulness.

☐ Every apostolate is an irradiation of Jesus Christ. It gives and explains something of Jesus Christ: doctrine by the apostolate of preaching, grace by the apostolate of the sacraments, formation by the apostolate of education, etc. Mary gives the whole Christ, Way, Truth and Life.

☐ Publishers possess the word. They multiply and distribute it in the form of paper, type and ink. On the human level, they have the mission that Mary had on another level. She was the Mother of the Eternal Word. She contained the invisible God and made him visible and accessible by presenting him in human form.

☐ Like a branch constantly bearing fruit, Mary always gives us Jesus, offering him to mankind as the Way, Truth and Life. She is the apostle of Jesus not by words only, but in mind, will and heart.

She always said what was necessary and essential: "fiat". Her actions were marked by constancy. Her entire will was committed; she lived by love. From the moment of the Annunciation, hers was an alert intelligence because of the Son she knew would be born of her. More than with ink, she wrote Jesus with her blood, that is, formed him within herself by the power of the Holy Spirit. In giving us Jesus, she gave us the Gospel. In giving us Jesus, she presented every perfection in him. In giving us Jesus, she gave us redemption, the Eucharist, life. "Hail, holy queen, mother of mercy our life, our sweetness and our hope . . .". Mary is, therefore, the apostle, the Queen of the Apostles, the exemplar of every apostolate, the inspiration of every apostolic virtue.

☐ We do not know enough yet about Mary as Queen of the Apostles. So true is this that I once heard this peculiar statement: in the image of the Queen of the Apostles, there is nothing referring to the apostolate. But isn't Mary depicted as giving Jesus? What more is the apostolate than the giving of Jesus? You do not distribute bread. You distribute truth, and by this you give Jesus to the world.

☐ Let us consecrate all of our houses, undertakings, schools and works of the apostolate to Mary. Hers is the office of forming and sustaining the apostles of all time and crowning their efforts with fruit. Mary enters the life of every sound vocation . . . and leads it towards Jesus. Novitiates and programmes of formation and study that are placed under her daily guidance bear abundant fruit. Our apostolates, in all their wide variety, receive light, strength, rectitude and assurance when they are totally coonsecrated to Mary.

5

St Paul today

In searching for the best guide to Christ's full mystery for the salvation of mankind, Father Alberione discovered St Paul. He made himself one of the most ardent disciples and imitators of the Apostle in modern times. Through his multi-form institutions and the media of social communication used as an apostolate, he strove to revive within the Church the figure of the Apostle of the Gentiles. What would St Paul do today? How would he love Christ in today's milieu? What would he do to announce the message to men of our time? Thus, St Paul became the patron of two of his Congregations, a number of churches, hundreds of book centres and film agencies, and many other apostolic works which he wanted to be nourished and sustained with the great openness and courage of the Pauline spirit.

☐

☐ The Pauline Family was raised up by St Paul as a means of continuing his work. St Paul is alive once more in the many members who are part of it. We did not choose St Paul. It was he who chose and called us. We must do what he would do if he were alive today. And if he were alive, what would he do? He would fulfill the two great commandments as he knew how to do so: loving God with all his heart, strength, and mind, and loving his neighbour unsparingly. This because he lived Christ: "Christ lives in me".

He would use the greatest pulpits of modern progress: the press, film, radio and television to announce the unparalleled message of love and salvation found in the Gospel of Jesus Christ. St Paul made himself our 'mould'.

☐ Before placing the Institute under the protection of the Apostle Paul, there was much prayer. A saint was needed who excelled in holiness and who at the same time would serve as an example for the apostolate. In himself, St Paul had integrated holiness and the apostolate. He truly loved Jesus Christ: "What can separate me from the love of Christ? Nothing. Neither life nor death". After having served Christ in life, he faced the martyrdom of beheading intrepidly. "Neither life nor death will separate me from Christ!" Before his ultimate witnessing to the Master, he gave his whole life to the apostolate. We often call attention to the activity of St Paul, but first we should call attention to his piety.

☐ St Paul is the disciple who knows the Divine Master in all his fulness. He lives him completely. He searches the profound mysteries of his teaching, his heart, holiness, humanity and divinity. He sees Christ as the supreme teacher, the host, the priest. He presents the total Christ as he had already defined himself: the Way, Truth and Life.

☐   If St Paul were alive today, he would still burn with the double flame of the same fire: zeal for God and his Christ, and zeal for men of every land. And in order to be heard, he would mount the most commanding pulpits and multiply his words with the current means of progress: the press, film, radio, television. His doctrine would not be cold or abstract. Whenever he reached a given place he did not give but an occasional conference. He stayed and he formed. He won intellectual consent, persuaded, converted, united people in Christ, started others on the road to a fuller Christian life. He did not leave until there was the moral certainty that his own would persevere. Presbyters would be left behind to continue his work but he communicated often by word and writing. He wanted to hear news of them, was with them in spirit, and prayed for them.

☐   The Letter of St Paul to the Romans is the first and principal example of the apostolate of communications, the example on which every Pauline production should be modelled. For this reason, when the church dedicated to St Paul was built at the motherhouse, it was decided to show the Apostle dictating his magnificent Letter to the Romans. In its totality, the sculpture ideally represents the spirit and purpose of our apostolate: to bring the Gospel to all peoples of every time.

☐   The whole secret of St Paul's greatness lies in his interior life. It can be said that he conquered from within: from his great spirit of poverty, study, profound knowledge, love of Jesus Christ, spirit of selflessness. In vain do we ask St Paul for the grace to become heroes before men. Our first need is to ask for the grace that will make us dear to God and only then for the grace to become apostles in the midst of the world.

Children must resemble their father. Every friend of St Paul must look to him and learn from his spirit. The more we read and are penetrated by the life and Letters of St Paul, the more we will love them, and the more we shall set out on a true path of sanctity, in the true spirit of the apostolate.

☐   The saint is not a burnt-out human being, a half-conscious

H

individual who doesn't quite know how to take his place in life. For St Paul, sanctity is the full maturity of the person.

The saint does not wrap himself up in introversion. He is open to development. He does not stay still. Rather, his motto is growth and progress.

Holiness is life, movement, nobility, dynamic enthusiasm. Not the kind that tapers off but the kind that soars upwards. But holiness will only and always be in proportion to our will-power and a spirit of faith. God is with us! We cooperate with him.

☐   I have told you St Paul wrote fourteen Letters. In twelve of them he reproves chatterboxes since those who talk too much disrupt the peace. Does this mean we shouldn't speak? No, it means to speak discerningly, at the right time and as necessity demands.

☐   There will be those who approve our apostolate and those who will not. However, you know that it is pleasing to God and useful to the Church. Know that this is what God has called us to. Forward with courage, then, remembering that "those who have worked, instructed others, will be called great in the kingdom of heaven".

Hold to the example of St Paul. He worked very hard and suffered very much in the exercise of his apostolate. Notwithstanding everything, he remained tireless up to the time he declared: "I have finished my course". If you, too, have exercised your apostolate with faith and zeal, you will be able to say at the end of your life: "I have accomplished the noble apostolate assigned to me, and now I await the reward".

☐   Vigilance and attention is necessary if the apostolate is to maintain the pastoral height found in the Letters of St Paul. The love of Jesus Christ and of souls will help us to distinguish and clearly separate what is apostolate and what is industry and business. The maximum criteria for judging things is always the spirit, whether the aspect involved is the intellectual, the moral, our poverty, or our apostolate. Great is the programme drawn from the Tabernacle: "From here I want to enlighten. Do not be afraid. I am with you. Be sorry for your sins".

6

The Word of God

In the spiritual life and in the apostolate, Father Alberione always served of the Bible as a lever. Biblical instruction, meditations inspired by the sacred text, the Gospel and the Letters of St Paul were the basis of the formation given by him to his religious family.

The Book of God displayed in every place of prayer, life and work, the publication of countless editions of the Gospel and that of Bible Week, the house-to-house propagation of the Word by the Daughters of St Paul, whom he loved to refer to as the 'postmistresses of God', the Visit before the Blessed Sacrament based on biblical reading — all of this recalls the fact that the font of Pauline spiritual thought and apostolic action was, and continues to be, the Word of God.

☐

☐ Believing souls know that every word and action of the Master contains a special grace which facilitates the practice of virtue in readers and hearers. They venerate the Word of God hidden beneath its outer appearance and they pray to be enlightened, to be able to understand, savour and practice its teachings. This reading is something of meditation and devout conversation with Jesus. And souls go away from this colloquy more resolved to follow him whom they admire and love.

☐ Those who read the Scriptures increase their faith. Those who prayerfully and frequently take this book into their hands and make of it their daily bread gradually become faith-oriented in their reasoning, faith-oriented in their judgements and aspirations. They become the kind of people described by the Holy Spirit: "The just person lives by faith".

☐ Love of the Gospel is the sign and characteristic of individuals whom God singles out for great undertakings.

☐ The Bible does not only teach us how to live well as individuals. Nor does it only teach us about domestic virtues, or only about what relates to religion. It also teaches us about all that can be grouped under the heading of social virtues.

The Bible teaches love among nations, love among the various social classes, the duties of owners towards employees and the duty of workers towards employers. It teaches justice and honesty in commerce and business, love for work, various forms of apostolate for the young, the elderly, the sick. It teaches the spiritual and corporal works of mercy.

☐ Would we ever have understood the meaning of humility,

gentleness, patience, the bearing of wrongs, virginity, and fraternal charity brought to the point of self-immolation if we had never read and meditated on the examples and lessons of our Lord?

Pagan philosophers, particularly the Stoics, wrote some beautiful pages about some of these qualities. But what a difference between their literary dissertations and the persuasive, powerful words of the Divine Master!

☐ The writer-apostle must conform to the Bible as the model book. God created man and knows very well how his heart is made. Therefore his word corresponds to the deepest needs of the human heart, much in the same way that a mother making clothes for her child tailors them to size.

☐ What can you give, therefore? God, and his word! How powerful you are when you cite a phrase from the Gospel! The Word of God is the highest authority. Who can object to God? We read in the psalms: "By reason of your word I am wiser and stronger than your enemies! Wiser than the elders who have studied and gained experience". Therefore, when you bring the word of God to others, and when your word is accompanied and strengthened by a scriptural phrase, who can find it unacceptable?

☐ Since we have to communicate the Lord's teaching, we must on one hand be very well enlightened, and on the other be able to convey the wisdom of God. We quote this and that author . . . Quote God! This is what God taught us! This is how Jesus Christ preached! At times we want to show how much we know . . . Let us show what God knows and what God taught. It was he who came to teach humanity. The truth which needs to be followed is the truth which he revealed in his preaching and teaching.

☐ The Bible is the book that we have to give, whether it be through film or print, through radio or records, through filmstrips or other forms. We present it through all the means that the Lord furnishes, just as we clothe and nourish ourselves with what he provides.

☐   These are promises that apostles of communications should make, especially those who are active in the editorial sector:
— *I promise* to honour the Gospel with the veneration that is its due;
— to give the Gospel complete deference of mind, will and heart;
— To consider the Gospel as the Truth, the Way, and the Life of my apostolate;
— to read the Gospel and meditate on it in the spirit of the Church;
— to spread it and work to multiply its copies in tireless love;
— to conform my entire life to it, wanting it near me in death and upon my breast in my coffin.

7

The Church —
the Pope

The Founder of the Pauline Family placed himself and the work that he had created at the service of the Church.

From the Church came the inspiration and approbation of his apostolic initiatives. His acute and profound sense of fidelity to the Church was also expressed in love and faithfulness to the Pope, Vicar of Christ, visible head of the Church. From Leo XIII to Paul VI, Father Alberione professed an enlightened devotion to the person and role of the Vicar of Christ. He resolutely transmitted this attitude to his sons and daughters, and succeeded in obtaining from the Holy See, for the Society of St Paul, the vow of 'fidelity to the Pope', as a sure guide for the practical exercise of the Pauline apostolate.

☐

☐ The Church, teacher of faith, morality and prayer, labours to form the perfect Christian, the citizen of heaven. This formation takes place in Christ who is the Way, the Truth and the Life. He made himself a teacher for our sake, and in the elevation, Christianization and divinization of man, he is the unique Master. Understanding this clearly, the Church, as the mystical body of Jesus Christ, labours wisely to communicate and perfect this education and formation of man, so as to make him a worthy part of Jesus Christ, the head. She continues his role as the incomparable Teacher.

☐ There is a sign that grows out of the perpetuity, authority and supernatural aspect of the Church. It is that in the varying circumstances of her history, the Church always finds the man who corresponds to the needs of the age. This man, anchored on the shores of eternity and lifted above changing events, is the Pope.

☐ We affirm our total affection, submission and dedication to the Pope. We are with the Pope in order to be with Jesus Christ.

☐ The Holy See has communities of religious at its service for general works. The overriding thought at this point is to have an ever more numerous corps, ever more spiritually and scientifically prepared, ever more closely joined to the Vicar of Jesus Christ, ever more prompt to respond to call, ever more tenacious in carrying out the work entrusted to each institute within the framework of its particular goals . . . We spend our lives well when we serve the Church, the Pope, and Jesus Christ in this way. Jesus Christ is the author, model, comfort and reward of religious.

☐ The authority of the hierarchy set us on a road and into an apostolate very different from the one ordinarily followed up to then. The Bishop of Alba summoned me one day and told me: "To your ordinary ministry I am now adding another and a quite demanding one". He indicated the path: the diocesan press. For the next twenty years, at high and low moments, he was to guide and sustain me on that path with wisdom and fortitude. From here everything else developed.

Now the two respected documents (of the Holy See) confirm how everything evolved under the light, guidance and approval of the Church, and more precisely, under "the Shepherd who guides the Church".

So the main thing is this: in Christ and in the Church always. This is how we started, and this is our life today.

☐   The Pauline Family came to be at a time when the reigning Holy Father had meagre support for many of his directives concerning the press. One of the aims of the Pauline Family was to make up for the lack of attention given to what the Pope was saying by a group of people who went ahead teaching as they saw fit and interpreting things according to their own point of view. They gave little heed to the one who had the obligation, duty and power to direct Catholics on the true path of the apostolate. Thus came *our vow of fidelity regarding the apostolate.*

☐   I besought His Holiness to hear me on two points that I had much at heart. Encouraged by him, I expressed a personal desire first. He reassured three times in regard to this, using words that were decisive and of great goodness.

Then I explained to the Holy Father how the prayer, study and apostolate of the Society of St Paul take their inspiration from the Divine Master, Way, Truth and Life. He very much approved and encouraged the hour of adoration practised in the Society of St Paul in honour of the Divine Master. Love for the only Master is also love for the universal, infallible, visible and indefectible teacher, who is the Pope. He blessed and encouraged this love, exhorting us to confirm, deepen and expand it. We were to take certain precise steps to make it increasingly more alive and practical in keeping with the spirit of the Church.

☐   In the apostolate, we must feel ourselves to be at the side of the Pope. It is for us to repeat what he teaches with the media that the Lord has given us. These are the same means indicated by the Second Vatican Council: the press, film, radio, television, and in general the technical media of social communication. We are to feel ourselves at the side of the Pope in his actions, to be at his service, to be at the side of the bishops and priests — to be of service, that is, in collaboration with and in dependence of the Church.

8

A great problem: vocations

Vocations to the priesthood and to the religious life constitute one of today's major problems for those who love the Church. Father Alberione knew that true vocations come from God, but that they call for the Church's concern and require the right circumstances and efforts in order to manifest themselves. For this problem to be resolved, a manner of thinking and acting that is unquestionably evangelical is needed, together with total dependence on God.

Father Alberione was instrumental in giving impetus to many priestly and religious vocations on various continents. He gave unreserved attention to this general problem of the Church, dedicating not only numerous writings to it but also one of his Congregations, the youngest of them: the Sisters of the Queen of the Apostles, founded for the vocations apostolate.

☐

☐ Among apostolic works, the problem of vocations occupies first place. Jesus did not begin his public ministry by preaching. He began it by making disciples. He looked for them along the lake shore and made his approach. James, John, Andrew, Peter, Philip and others responded.

☐ The Lord made man free. A vocation is an act of love on God's part. It begs a voluntary act of love to be followed and corresponded to. A vocation finds its model in Jesus Christ, who said to the Father: "Here I am, O God, to do your will".

☐ The needs of humanity, of the Church, and of souls are immense. One readily understands why so many projects and works are proposed. But works are done when there are people to do them. And these people are productive in the measure that they are grafted into Christ. Electric current has high and low tension. Religious life is spiritual current at high tension. It is the poetry of a personality in Christ, who is the generator and promoter of heroism. Thus the necessity for vocations in every religious and ecclesial sector, as reflected in the papal associations fostering vocations to the diocesan clergy and religious communities. The Institute of the Queen of the Apostles is a response to this need. Its line of action for vocations conforms to the teaching and example of Jesus Christ, Way, Truth and Life. A sufficient number of good vocations constitutes the greatest need of the Church today in every part of the world.

☐ Truly loving our neighbours as ourselves, we would want for many others the great good that we possess: our vocation. If we are happy to have received this grace, we want others to share it. If our mind is bent towards sanctity, we yearn for others, too, to live this ideal.

☐   Just remunerator that he is, God rewards those who always do his will. Discerning the will of God is at once simple and complicated, clear and obscure, sad and sweet, and depending on individual cases, natural and marvellous. Let there not be, therefore, a casual attitude, nor exasperation or tormented uncertainty but, rather, prudence, examen, prayer, counsel and decisions made in faith.

Where innocence and a proper environment prevails, the call of the Lord often manifests itself soon after the age of reason. Sometimes it entails coming out of a forest of obscurity and into the light of the sun, out of a sorrow or disappointment, out of a scarring worldly experience. "Come, follow me," is the persuasive invitation. Out of a shattering event to a horizon filled with hope. Out of a lazy, carefree, extravagant life to a thirst for sacrifice. "The Spirit breathes where it wills."

☐   If our apostolate truly follows God the Writer and Publisher, it will endure and bear fruit. Vocations will multiply. Vocations come to us when it is obvious that we are giving people the wisdom of God. They leave us when they don't see this. To give God to humanity: let this be our anxious sigh, our daily prayer.

☐   Cooperate with the Heavenly Father not only in making a cage but likewise in searching for the birds. When we say, "Give us a nest for ourselves", we mean to ask for both bird and cage. Vocations are immensely more numerous than those who come. May none be lost because of us!

Before all else, pray. Then invite, foster, work, do something. There is still laziness in this field, indifference, lukewarmness. Those who really love the Institute prove it by trying to contribute to its good. And the first good of a family are its persons. Numerous, good persons.

☐   Maybe we say, "Come and follow me", because we have a nice house. Or because we have such and such an apostolate. Or because there are possibilities for study . . . Why these human motivations? "Come and follow me", because you will have an eternal reward. Say it clearly: "If anyone wants to be a follower of mine, let him deny himself daily, take up his cross and follow me".

9

The Priest

Father Alberione was essentially a priest, and his manifold works sprang basically from a vivid awareness of his priestly commitment.

Making the priesthood the cornerstone of all the Pauline apostolic institutions, he gave it a new dimension by introducing it into the field of the media of social communication. He sought for numerous religious brothers to collaborate with this priesthood, elevating them, in his words, to a 'quasi-priesthood'. He did the same for women, in accord with the guidelines expressed in a book written in his early priesthood on the role of women associated with the work of priests.

In the current crisis of priestly renewal, it is a bracing experience to feel this man's ardent faith in the mission of the priesthood.

☐

☐ We adore Jesus Christ the Priest, to whom every priest is joined in one priesthood, the Letter to the Hebrews tells us.

We thank Jesus Christ the Priest, in whom, for whom, and with whom we glorify the Holy Trinity.

We make atonement to Jesus Christ the Priest for the betrayals that have followed down the centuries since the time of Judas.

We pray to Jesus Christ the Priest that every age will have a sufficient number of priests who will make themselves the light of the world, the salt of the earth, the city on the mountaintop.

☐ The existence, quality and value of our priesthood rests on that of Jesus Christ. Needing to apply the fruits of his oblation in time and space, Jesus Christ chose to use instruments who would lend their hands, tongue and purpose. He absorbed and took them to be his own, working through them ...

Our priestly being is united to his. All our strength, power and grace derive from the high priest of our religion. There is no other sacrifice and no other true high priest.

☐ I am a miracle of God! Your infinite mercy has brought me to the priesthood: "By the grace of God, I am what I am".

Ordination transformed the twelve. Ordination made me a new being, God on earth.

I identify with Christ. His interests are my interests, his intentions are mine. I speak his words, my doctrine is his, my life is Christ's. I do his work, or better, he does it in me. "Peter baptizes, but it is Christ who baptizes; Judas baptizes, but it is Christ who baptizes." I am obligated to God. I must live as Jesus Christ lived.

☐ The priest cannot be a man who lives for himself. His motto cannot be: I am God. It is absolutely necessary that he work for the salvation of others and that his coat-of-arms be: I-God-People.

☐ The director's secret is nothing other than directing, that is, having a priestly mind, soul and heart in resolute journey towards heaven, indicating the road, inspiring and drawing a multitude behind . . .

Direct truly, as Jesus Christ did. He completely made himself the Way, Truth and Life! This is not simply a method, philosophy or moral teaching, but the method, the philosophy, the moral teaching, the apostolate, the secret — in keeping with man and revelation in keeping with nature and grace.

We are not florists but gardeners. We are other Christs, not just echoes. We are the salt, not vendors of salt. We are the light, not its reflectors. We are the city posted on the mountaintop, not its discoverers. We recruit the faithful in the struggle against sin, but we lead them as captains at the head of the army. We are the motors, not just the trailers. We resolutely strive for heaven, not just point it out to others. We are not merely spectators, but gladiators in the arena, indeed, squad-leaders reaching for the reward. We are not sheeplike followers, nor marchers in a parade, but wise guides and shepherds of the flock of Christ and of the Church.

☐ O priest-writers, let us write after Mass and allow ourselves to be channels by which the blood of Christ passes from his heart to fill our own and then overflows towards our readers.

Let us understand the yearning, sighing, thirsting spirit of Jesus for men, and become his ardent voice calling, insisting, pleading and entreating in all patience and doctrine.

O priest-writers, the fruit of what you do depends more on your knees than on your pen, more on your Mass than on your technique, more on your examination of conscience than on your knowledge!

The lay writer is a reflector of light. You must show him the way and give him life. Speak out incessantly as St John the Baptist and St Paul did. Call attention to sin, let your virtue be seen, communicate by the strength of the Holy Spirit and that of your example.

☐ The priest who is learned is esteemed. The priest who is powerful is feared. The priest who speaks well is listened to. But only the priest steeped in great charity is loved.

I

☐   A priest cannot claim to be satisfied with himself by reason of splendid ceremonies in church, the perfection of congregational hymn singing, the practice of a thousand devotions, etc. He cannot content himself with certain types of pilgrimages and processions that resemble more a parade or march. Nor that people admire his eloquence in preaching, or that others dwell lingeringly on concepts that are very spiritual. He cannot even be satisfied if all, or nearly all, are fulfilling their Easter duty, are being married in church, are asking for a Christian funeral etc. These things are means. The goal is to change human thinking into Christian thinking, to transform human affection into Christian affection, human works into those that are worthy of a Christian. A person must be a Christian not by reason of baptism alone, nor only in church. But at home, in his family and in society, everywhere and in all things.

☐   Every priest who reads the Acts of the Apostles with a spirit of faith, and the life of St Paul and his Letters, cannot help but become aware of new dimensions for his ministry and new horizons for his sanctification. A parish priest's familiar meeting with the Apostle of the Gentiles will enchant him. He will be moved to admiration and imitation, for St Paul is ever in vogue.

☐   Jesus, Divine Master, may your amiable heart be thanked and praised for the institution of the priesthood. As you were sent by the Father, so priests are sent by you. You have charged them with the treasures of your doctrine, your precepts, your grace, and souls themselves. Help me to love them, listen to them, and allow myself to be guided by them. Send good labourers into your vineyard, O Jesus. May priests be the salt which purifies and preserves, the light of the world, the city on the mountaintop. May all of them resemble you in heart. May they be surrounded one day in heaven with a multitude of conquered souls, their crown and joy.

10

The Brother,
disciple of the Divine Master

In his anxiety to "restore all things in Christ", and to be inspired in all things by the Gospel, Father Alberione conceived his institution on the model of the Family of Nazareth, as well as on the apostolic community which followed the Divine Master in Palestine. Therefore, at the side of priests who continue the life of Jesus as heirs of the apostles, he envisioned the 'disciples', imitators of St Joseph and of the seventy-two who were also sent to preach the message of salvation. In this way, the religious who was not a priest was to participate in the same priestly ministry not just through executive cooperation but by an original contribution offering him a vital role in a modern apostolate. "Priests and disciples (brothers) carry out the same apostolate together . . . and therefore merit the name of apostles."

Here we clearly see the careful profile of the non-priestly vocation developed by Father Alberione. He restored the original features of the evangelical workers to it, consecrated as they are to the same apostolic activity as their brother-priests.

☐   Man is always a disciple of God. Through creation, human history, the gift of reason, revelation, and the ongoing action of the Holy Spirit in the Church, God is the great teacher of man.

☐   According to the Latin word *discere*, 'disciple' defines someone who is learning. In our case, it signifies "a learning of him who is wisdom, truth and life: Jesus Christ".

☐   There are many generous souls in the world whom the Lord calls to himself for perfection and to work hand-in-hand with the priesthood. Who will have the charity to open a door of special holiness to them? . . . And why may they not also be associated with an apostolate? In other times, institutes rose up in which priest-religious found the way open to varying zealous works in the care of souls. Today why not give brother-religious a participation in priestly work? Why not give him a quasi-priesthood. . . ? Let priests and brothers be united in the same apostolate while preparing for heaven.
So it is that we have disciples (brothers). Priestly preaching with the modern means frees them from the drudgery of common labour and aids its indefinite multiplication. The work of the brother is elevating, joyous, varied. God is glorified through it, the Gospel is announced, and light is brought to people.

☐   The brother-disciple is modelled on St Joseph. He is at the priest's side in formation to cooperate with him in the apostolate. The most important aspect of this cooperation is in being at the priest's side in prayer. This works for his own sanctification . . .

☐   Like St Joseph, the brothers carry out an arduous work in cooperating for the coming of the kingdom of God. Their path of sanctification is similar to his. They find fulfilment in a spirit of piety, in humble conformity to the will of God, in unassuming labour and toil. They blend the contemplative and active life. Their apostolate is broad, modern, satisfying . . .

In this marvellous mission, young men can find a place in which to spend their intellectual, spiritual and physical energies well. All the technical aspects of publishing and marketing, film-making, the book centres, etc., present them with a splendid and varied field of apostolate.

☐ When the technical means of the press, cinema, radio, tele-vision, etc., are used in the service of evil, they do great harm. This spectacle is enough to fire the heart of an apostle.

The brother-disciple of the Divine Master makes not only a negative reparation for this, but one that is altogether positive. It consists in the direct exercise of the social communications aposto-late: opposing the press with the press, film with film, radio with radio, television with television. It involves confronting error with truth, evil with good, Satan with Jesus Christ.

☐ If the brother's life is rightly presented to upright young men, or to adults familiar with the vanity of the world and deluded by the taste of it, if it is presented to them in its form of modern activity, articulated in its purely evangelical spirituality, demon-strated in an apostolate carried out in recollection while aimed at hundreds of thousands of persons, it will attract a great number of candidates. Well informed, they will walk the fulfilling road of the great commandments: "Love the Lord . . . Love your neigh-bour as yourself".

11

Women associated with priestly ministry

Thousands of women have followed the paths opened up by Father Alberione. Like him, their ideal has been "to do something for the Lord and humanity" in their time.

The Congregations of the Daughters of St Paul, Sister Disciples of the Divine Master, Pastorelle Sisters, Queen of the Apostles Sisters, and the secular institute of Our Lady of the Annunciation, have given young women of thirty nations the possibility of associating themselves with the pastoral apostolate of the priesthood, and in this way, of responding to the spiritual needs of mankind today.

From the pages of the Gospel and from his own clear insight into the marvellous resources of the feminine soul for collaborating in the Kingdom of Christ, Father Alberione learned to understand women and speak to them.

☐

☐   The designs of God the creator for women, confirmed by God redeemer, continue to unfold and be realized through a winding history of anguish, impediment, and small and great heroism. Womanhood's ideal, as resplendent in Mary, is more and more considered by all of humanity. Woman is the helpmate of man and similar to him. With him she forms one body. With him she receives and applies redemption in the Church. With him she works for the social and moral elevation of man.

☐   Woman can hold the world in her hand!

☐   Today's woman must form today's man. She must assist in meeting the needs of today's man, using today's means.

☐   It is necessary to reflect on the contribution that woman can make to the Church and to humanity by reason of the strength and dedication natural to her. This is the reason why the Pauline Family was not intended for men alone. The Lord willed that it be composed of women also.

☐   Woman appears complete to us when she combines: culture and spirituality, family and society, the ability to make an effective contribution to civil and religious works, the capacity to give herself to God and belong to him completely, while belonging to man so as to complete him. She is the weaker sex, yet what power in that supplicating weakness! Wisely advised, there is no heroism beyond her reach. Humiliated and cast aside, she has the strength to get back on her feet and rebuild a new future on the foundation of Christian hope.

☐   The apostolate of preaching by the written word is very much adapted to women. In the Church, women do not have the mandate but are its very effective collaborators.

How many catechists, lecturers and able mothers know how to teach children well! How many women know how to educate in a manner that is telling and penetrating, transforming their surroundings! Because a woman is a natural mother, she can adapt to and influence all hearts, either in the family or society.

☐   Every religious sister, especially you who are constantly exposed to the public eye, must be a living book by which 'readers' may learn the imitation of Christ, how to live as God intends, how the Gospel is translated into practice.

☐   Distribute the Scriptures. It is God's letter written to man, but there are few to deliver it. The Daughters of St Paul are its postmistresses. The Scriptures need multiplying and the Daughters of St Paul aid in this. What beautiful things you have to do! God has written, but people do not receive his letter. It is for you to deliver it as widely as possible. If you are effective as postmistresses of God, be assured that you will have found the path that leads to heaven!

12

Fundamental choice:
religious life

In his private notes, Father Alberione wrote of himself:

"In 1910 he took a definite step: there would be writers, technicians, distributors, but they would be *religious* men and women. On the one hand, they would be brought to the highest perfection through the practice of the evangelical counsels joined to the merit of apostolic life. On the other hand, they would bring more unity, stability, continuity, and a sense of the supernatural to the apostolate. An organization would be formed, but a religious one, where energies would be joined, where dedication would be total, where doctrine would be more sound. And this society of souls, loving God with all their mind, strength and heart, would spend themselves in work for the Church, content with the divine stipend: 'Receive a hundredfold and possess life everlasting'. He rejoiced, therefore, considering part of this army of souls as belonging to the Church on earth, and part as belonging to the Church in heaven."

From then on, having this goal before him to be attained — an apostolate with modern means — the overriding theme of his priestly work and thought became the religious life.

☐

☐ The religious life has its roots deep in the Gospel. Christianity is always passed over by the world as a living paradox, a madness to some, a scandal to others. For us it is divine truth and reality, as attested to in the eight beatitudes pronounced by the Divine Master.

The religious state, which is a perfecting of the Christian life and integral practice of the Gospel, seems all the more a paradox: the sacrifice of one's life in order to save it, the loss of everything in order to win all. And in culmination of this paradox, poverty becomes wealth, abasement leads to exaltation, virginity bears life, servitude becomes freedom, sacrifice—beatitude, service—apostolate, death—life. "You are dead and your life is hidden with Christ in God." "I have been crucified with Christ, and if I am alive, it is no longer I who live but Christ who lives in me." The mystic crucifixion of the religious is accomplished by the three nails of poverty, chastity and obedience.

After the Mass and martyrdom, this is the greatest and most meritorious act. Each morning, during the renewal of the Eucharistic Sacrifice, I fasten my whole being to his same cross and renew the three vows.

☐ More than ever before, this age calls for religious. If they are well chosen and prepared, it is from them that the Church will draw immense advantage in every aspect of its universal activity. Throughout its millennium of history and in its most turbulent periods, it has always been this way. Tempered by deep piety, study and observance, religious emerged from their silence, took up places in front lines, and led the way towards a civilization that was Christian and Catholic. Today the needs are of incalculable breadth and depth.

☐ Religious life may be exposed to tremendous trials in the next generation if it is not sustained by a strong and genuine faith.

☐   One state or another, one order or another, one institute or another becomes extinct because of lack of members or lack of religious spirit. But the religious state itself can never disappear or diminish in value, since it pertains to the integrity of the Church. It is its external image, and one of the principal characteristics of its holiness. Is this our concept of it?

☐   The religious does not have a series of promotions to allure him. His aim is not recognition or the bearing of titles. Religious are not after esteem or distinction. They do not have the worry of a salary. Their trust is in the hundredfold, reaping a hundred times more than what they have given up.

As the Holy Spirit gives us light and as much as it lies within our choice, we should prefer humiliation to praise, poverty to possessions, thanklessness to recognition, suffering to consolation and well being. Let us consider ourelves indebted to all. Before the diocesan clergy, let us take second place.

Let us be ready to bring the faith to people, to build up parishes, to be organizers in a diocese . . . and then be prepared to hand it all over to the local clergy. When everything is flowing smoothly in the Church, let us attend to prayer, study, ministry and apostolate. But when the Church is ploughing through troubled waters, let us come forward and make an active and prayerful contribution. The moment passed, let us retreat to the shadows, disposed to accept misunderstanding or harsh criticism because more was expected of us. Demands will be made on us and no exchange given. To confess, to preach, to minister without recompense; to spend long and heavy hours in editorial work or in the apostolate, at times to the detriment of our health, to be looked on as loafers or business-people: all this is what the religious chooses and accepts with his profession . . .

But there is the hundredfold, and, if one is faithful, life eternal.

☐   Observe the kind of mystery there is in profession: poverty is the greatest wealth, chastity is the greatest love, obedience is the greatest freedom.

☐   Charity in obedience and obedience in charity! Internal divisions in an institute have serious consequences: divisions in thought, direction, character, teaching, work, etc. They destroy the spirit and life of the institute at its foundations. Union is such a vital element as to merit the sacrifice of particular points of view and particular advantages.

☐   There are individuals who take over the ship and impose themselves on the community. Others without discernment or control, follow and applaud. One such person is enough to topple morale.

Superiors should encourage members to reflect and be guided by principles. They should try to counsel docility in individuals, without going to the excesses of infantilism. How many religious are subject to group pressure, to exaggerated or de-personalizing influences! To grow as a healthy person, one must know how to be alone at times, to decide for oneself, in a word, to behave as an adult. Decisiveness, vigour, tenacity and sound principles will result in the best religious, the best teachers, the best spiritual directors.

☐   A bolt of cloth, even two thousand yards long, is always the end product of small threads. It is this way with our life. However long, it is made up of minutes, and the sanctifying of minutes is the secret of holiness. Most of our activities as religious do not require heroism. Heroism, instead, lies in being constant in the practice of theological virtue, in living each moment well. Don't be fitful in your religious life: now going full steam, now paused, now back-pedalling. No! Constant small steps every single day.

☐   In humility and confidence, we have to go forward without pause. Humility is our left foot, confidence our right. Let us use both of them to walk as we should.

☐   In short, I want you to be whole persons, not propped up manikins. Isn't this what you want? You must tell yourselves: I myself want to earn heaven. And then, onwards — without a lot of nonsense!

☐   Sin lies in the body. It is a profound aberration and humiliates the whole of man, his mind, will, heart and body. Behind the law of mortification lies life.

The greatest battles must be fought, and won or lost, in the hidden recesses of the mind. There are no witnesses to encourage or disapprove. Only God sees thoughts. Self-reflection and examination of conscience bring some of these to light. But it is through true spiritual direction and the confessional that they are manifested and discerned. It is in the mind that the edifice of good is erected, or that pitiful ruins pile up.

☐   Institutes will flourish in the measure that they are faithful to the interior life and to their specific apostolate.

☐   No one can hate a child; innocence is transparent in his eyes. When one is guileless in this way, he has great power over others. Persons who are controlled are followed and exert much influence on hearts and souls for the sake of the Lord. Whoever is mortified and attains self-dominion has power over others, because no one has greater strength than one who has mastered himself. "It is a greater thing to have mastered oneself than to have conquered cities."

☐   There is a cloister that depends on us and deserves more attention than a community enclosure. When malice exists, you can close every door, raise every wall, install every alarm, and it will still not be enough! It is the heart that needs enclosure and guarding. Precautions prescribed and recommended by Church law and the Constitutions must be taken seriously, of course. To examine and guide the heart is of the highest importance.

13

Prayer

Father Alberione's words on prayer were matched by a vital personal practice of lifelong intensity and emphasis. All who lived with him recall him as exceptionally exemplary on this point.

His words on prayer were mainly directed to religious, particularly to those consecrated to the apostolate of the means of social communication — they had special need of an intense relationship with God in order to maintain the force of their apostolate always intact. "From contemplation to action."

One of the specific forms of prayer that he strongly recommended to the Pauline Family was a daily hour before the Lord in the Eucharist. He saw this hour as a kind of learning period with Christ the Divine Master, Way, Truth and Life. It was especially in this encounter with the Lord that Father Alberione hoped for the realization, in each member, of the central idea of Pauline spirituality: the full development of the human person in Christ in keeping with his resources of mind, will, heart and physical strength. And this until the basic experience of St Paul would become a fact: "I live, not I; it is Christ who lives in me."

☐

☐ Those who do not put prayer in the very first place do not deserve the name of religious, and in fact are not.

☐ Our prayers place all of our being before God: mind, will, heart, body. They come from the basic sources of the Church and are meant to form the religious-apostle while retaining their strong and devout sentiment. One who is familiar with them and is faithful to them will gradually be illumined, fortified and guided in the spirituality of St Paul.

☐ True piety pervades our whole being with love of God. It achieves the purpose of the first commandment: love the Lord with all your mind, heart and will.

☐ The first and foremost duty of man, of the Christian, of the religious and priest, is prayer. We can give no greater contribution to the Congregation than prayer. No work is more useful for us than prayer. No priestly work is more profitable for the Church than prayer. Therefore, prayer must be before all, above all, and the life of all.

The temptation may come: I have much work to do, too much work. But the primary work for you, the supreme mandate of the priest, the main contribution to be made to the Congregation, is that of prayer.

It is an illusion for some to excuse their lack of prayer on the pretext that they are too busy.

Is this really the reason? Or is it that we find our work-load heavy because it is not preceded by prayer? Prayer makes it easier to get many things done.

Too busy? But the Church, the Congregation, our own souls beg prayer — after which attending to whatever is possible.

Too busy? Yes, but in general our tasks are not more urgent than prayer.

Too busy? First God, then men.

Too busy? But the life of what we do is grace. Without prayer, therefore, what we do is dead.

"Cursed is the study, apostolate, etc., for which we give up prayer."

☐ "But there are things that need to be done, calls that must be made." Reply: organize everything well; but in the order of action, prayer is to precede. Once prayer is made, do all that you can. And in the case of the impossible, cut back on your zealous work. During the early years of ministry, there are those who unthinkingly empty themselves of whatever they had accumulated during the years of novitiate and study. And then? The salt becomes insipid and as such no longer seasons.

Objection: but we have to give ourselves to souls! Precisely. A mother eats to keep herself in full health and have abundant milk for her children. It is charity for our neighbour that makes us care for ourselves. "Indeed, doing this you will save yourself and those who hear you."

If we pray, we will surely be of benefit to others; we shall obtain the favours of God for them.

☐ Is our prayer something total? To separate apostolate from prayer is like living with a paralyzed limb, or a crucial part of us cut off from its bloodstream. This matter is so important as to merit a month's meditation. But a start can be made by making a good examination of conscience. Is our prayer vital? Does it influence our life? Or is it rather like an object forgotten in a drawer and left unused?

☐ First and foremost, our piety is Eucharistic. From this vital source, the Eucharistic Master, everything is given life. This is how the Pauline Family was born, before the Tabernacle. From here it is sustained in life, work and holiness. Our sanctity and apostolate spring from the Mass, Communion, the Eucharistic Visit.

☐   On one hand, the offering of prayer is among the most fundamental of duties towards God, and on the other, it is indispensable for obtaining the grace necessary for eternal salvation.

To impregnate all of our life, preaching, publishing and education with this conviction will bring great merit, clear illumination, and indispensable strength.

Before this world which hails achievement, power and knowledge, we have to preach this truth, and further, witness to it in prayer. The world, the Church and souls have a supreme need of God. Prayer brings him to us.

☐   When one's piety is abundant and wise, it will be easy to utilize our talents, be they many or few. Knowledge, apostolate, or poverty, on their own, without piety will not enlighten or kindle our ardour.

☐   We must pray, pray, pray. If our prayer is deep, all the better. But should we encounter distraction, we still must pray. And whoever perseveres at it will obtain what he asks — like the man in the Gospel who had recourse to his friend for bread in the middle of the night.

Whoever prays every day gains the grace to pray better. Whoever prays, personally admits a need for God and trusts that his prayer will be heard. As long as we persist in humble supplication, we demonstrate our faith, hope and charity. And before rising from our prayer, we will have already obtained divine blessings. In other words, just as we constantly take food and constantly breathe, all of us, every day of our lives, must truly pray.

☐   The liturgy is like a river of grace, light and blessing flowing through the year. It is for us to penetrate and understand it well. To have the spirit of the liturgy means that we be attuned to the praying Church and pray with the Church.

14

The constructive meaning of poverty

One of the prominent characteristics of Father Alberione's thought and activity is an emphasis on poverty in his religious family. Clearly maintaining the gospel sense of poverty as detachment, that is, a total liberty of spirit so as to love without reserve, Father Alberione decisively espouses the Pauline concept of evangelical poverty, *work*, which engages all the energies of life. This inserts poverty into the effort of developing the integral human person, who is called today to a specific Christian witness. It leads each one to spend every energy in charity while concretely developing the apostolic organization of the means of social communication. In this way, poverty tends to become a decisively constructive element, indispensable to the equilibrium of the Institute and of individuals. "Ours is a vehicle that moves on four wheels: piety, study, apostolate, poverty."

☐

☐ Poverty guarantees an institute's sound spirit and development, plus the blessing of good and numerous vocations.

God does not send candidates where people do not work or where there is waste, however insignificant. To be attached to even a strand of thread is like being a bound bird. His flight will not be launched towards the summits of holiness.

☐ All institutes are committed to poverty though not in the same way. The poverty of a Cistercian is one thing; that of a Jesuit, another. The norm of St Thomas holds: "Religious poverty is of instrumental value in achieving the double end for which it was meant: santification and apostolate".

☐ St Paul points out that those who compete in races do not weigh themselves down with pack and baggage. They dress lightly so as to cover as much ground as quickly as possible. Religious who truly love poverty run more rapidly towards heaven. There are men who love humility but not humiliation, and poverty but not privation. If sacrifice has to be made, they are no longer to be found. They are happy to do nothing, which is contrary to poverty. Jesus taught about poverty not so much by word as by example.

☐ For as long as he finds himself in full vigour, the religious who has reached final profession should provide for the support of at least three or four persons. He ought to make up for the expenses sustained in his formation, for those of other candidates, for the needs of his later years. Isn't this the obligation that fathers of families shoulder?

☐ The Institute must be poor and rich at the same time — poor in our personal observance of poverty, rich in the means we have of apostolate.

☐ Pauline poverty has five functions: to renounce, produce, preserve, provide and edify.

It renounces the independent administration and use of goods. It renounces comfort, pleasure and preferences. Everything is for use only.

It produces by diligent work. It produces for the support of our works and personnel.

It preserves the things that are in use.

It provides for the needs of the Institute.

It edifies, countering the tendency to greed.

☐ Institutes begin with works of zeal, but after a time, gain is sought. Within fifty or sixty years, hospices that were originally opened for the poor give precedence to those who can pay more. And the poor find themselves in the same condition as before. A school is opened for the education of destitute children, and gradually becomes a private school accepting only those who can afford a high tuition. In this way, needy students and the less fortunate are commercialized.

The means of life are necessary, of course. But the nature of the Institute is not to be changed! There was no need for a religious Institute to set up a business! There was no need for persons consecrated to God to be caught up in commerce!

☐ The whole of the Gospel moves about in the world of labour. Everyone has this obligation! No one is exempt, even if he is rich. The parable of the talents shows this. Work is also the means of subsistence compensated by a just wage. Work is ennobling and redemptive.

☐ A God who redeems the world by domestic virtue and thirty years of hard work — redemptive work, apostolic work, exhausting work! Isn't this the way of holiness: to put all our energies, even the physical, into the active service of God? Isn't God purest act? Isn't it here that the religious poverty of Jesus Christ truly shows itself? Shouldn't religious, more so than others, fulfil the duty of earning their own bread? Wasn't this the rule that

St Paul imposed upon himself? Isn't this the social duty that must be performed before an apostle presents himself to preach? Doesn't this make us humble? For the Pauline Family, isn't the apostolate of pen-in-hand as essential as that of the 'pen' of the machine? Isn't work healthy? Doesn't it protect us against laziness and temptation? Isn't it fitting that offerings and donations go only towards new projects (i.e., a church or equipment for the apostolate), and for the poor and vocations? If Jesus Christ took this road, wasn't it because this was one of the first things to restore? Isn't work a means of merit? If our Family works, doesn't it establish itself in the life of Christ in an essential way?

☐ To provide bread is a good deed. But when we are dealing with youth and persons active in work, to teach them to earn their bread is a deed doubly valid and doubly meritorious.

☐ It is dangerous to be weighed down by debts that are disproportionate to income. This can create a situation of anxiety and economic pressure that may bear heavily on the community's spirit, apostolate and study, while consuming all the benefits of the apostolate. It is equally harmful, however, not to provide what is positively necessary for spirit, health, apostolate, study and dignified living quarters. . . We have moments that are comparable to the life of the Holy Family in Bethlehem and Egypt, moments comparable to Nazareth, and to the public life of the Divine Master.

If houses, equipment, etc., are acquired intelligently and employed diligently, they will easily pay for themselves.

☐ You don't have to be told that the 'I press forward' of St Paul does not mean to press forward in prices! These should be aimed at the minimum possible, that is, the lowest price or the least possible offering that will permit the apostolate to go ahead, and the Congregation to live and accomplish its specific work.

15

Apostolate:
radiating Christ

The apostolate is the end for which Father Alberione brought the Pauline Family into being. With it, there came a great many creative activities by which the Word of God was presented in current forms.

The apostolate is thus the background for all his thoughts. Guided by St Paul, he continually studied its content, its source and the spiritual vigour needed to sustain it. On the nature of the apostolate, therefore, Father Alberione etches this profound concept: its indispensable and continual derivation from Christ, the only Saviour of mankind. This fact demands an attitude of life which vitally blends contemplation and action, the love of God and the love of man.

☐ The apostle is one who carries God within his soul and irradiates him to others.

The apostle is a saint who accumulates treasure and gives it in surplus to mankind.

The apostle has a heart glowing with the love of God and the love of humanity, and can neither restrain or suffocate what he feels and thinks.

The apostle is a vessel of election that overflows; those who long to quench their thirst follow him.

The apostle is a temple of the triune God, who is supremely active in him. To quote from a writer, he exudes God from all his pores: with word, work, prayer, gestures, attitudes, whether in public or in private; he gives his entire being.

Live by God! And give God.

☐ How many times do you ask yourself the great question: where is mankind heading, how is it moving, towards what goal is it aiming as it successively renews itself on the face of the earth? Humanity is like a great river flowing into eternity. Will it be saved? Will it be lost forever?

☐ Don't be frantic with worry trying to get rid of the darkness. Simply turn on some light.

☐ Sterile tears shed about present evils hardly give glory to God, nor do they benefit man. "Go and do likewise", as the Samaritan did. He was not content just to look at the man beaten and robbed. He bent to give him help, found him shelter, and paid his expenses. . .

☐ How is it possible to love Jesus and not yearn for his words to reach the whole world?

How is it possible to keep up the effort of the apostolate without strength from the Eucharist, our spiritual nourishment? You would have had good reason to complain had the apostolate not been linked to the Eucharist. It would have been like sending you to work sick and infirm.

Before growing cold in the apostolate, people grow cold in their devotion to the Eucharist. When there are mistakes in the apostolate, it is always because Eucharistic devotion is not very much alive.

Prudence, simplicity, zeal, love of the Church, the glory of God and the peace of men emanate from the Eucharist.

☐ If all the equipment of our printing plants were functioning but the electric power shut off, no matter how new and impressive the machines, they would count for nothing. "But it's a question of a thread of a wire and hardly visible!" Very well, try to operate without it, if you can!

Grace is spiritual power obtained through the sacraments and prayer. If Christians didn't have Communion, they would repent having known their religion, not then being able to practise it. There are some who have a great love for conferences and the opportunity to appear learned. Others loudly inveigh against vices, and believe they have done a lot. No, no, this is not enough. We have to give Jesus in his entirety!

☐ Piety is the soul of the apostolate. An apostolate without a soul is dead, and as such contributes nothing to the life of the one who performs it, nor to others. God summons you to the apostolate, and it is he who endows it with grace.

☐ Every apostolate is worthwhile. But the cross and passion redeemed the world. When we have learned to join the apostolate of suffering to the apostolate of communications, then Redemption is integrally offered. "I complete in my flesh whatever is lacking to the sufferings of Christ for the good of his body, the Church." "Without the shedding of blood, there is no remission (of sin)."

☐   To participate in the Mass with a social conscience is to transform it into a living apostolate.

☐   The distribution of books and periodicals is not effective until it brings people to reconciliation and Communion. The fundamental point is this: to unite them to Jesus. Always aim at this.

☐   This is the apostolate: to be both virgins and mothers. The more souls are pure or purified, the more will Mary's apostolate be carried out and made timely and fruitful.

Whether living or dying, healthy or sick, serving others or having to be served, it is always possible for us to give Jesus to the world and carry out an apostolate. Some do this in one way, others in another. But the *duty* of spiritual motherhood must be felt by all, the duty of giving Jesus to the world.

☐   Sow, sow! It is true that it is tiresome to sow seeds. But there is joy in the harvest. In death, the thought that you have exercised your apostolate well will bring you great consolation.

☐   The apostolate supposes a spirit of sacrifice, whether this be of money, health, time or esteem. It entails disappointments, criticism, opposition, and often from where this is least expected. It may even come from the very individuals for whose eternal health we are labouring, or from whom we have received help.

☐   Suffering is not only a trial but an apostolate. It is a secret of joy; it is participation in the redemptive work of the Saviour.

16

Apostolate with the means of social communication

"Ancient spirit, new forms." This was the operative principle of Father Alberione as he strove to fulfil the mission entrusted to him by God. The ancient spirit was that of the Gospel, of St Paul, of the best tradition of the Church. The new forms were those suggested by human progress in the twentieth century for the influence of the masses and mutual relations among men: the press, motion pictures, radio, television — that is, the means of social communication. With admirable ease and courage, Father Alberione entered this field and gave it an authentic stamp of apostolate. He stands in the Church as a master in the use of these forms of the Christian apostolate — difficult forms that are undergoing continual evolution.

☐

☐   We have always to lead others towards heaven. But we must lead those who live today, not those who lived ten or more centuries ago. We have to take the world and mankind as they are *today*, in order to do good *today*.

☐   Apostolate means bringing humanity its salvation: Jesus Christ, Way, Truth and Life.

The Pauline apostolate is universal in time and place.

With modern means, it preaches what the Pope, bishops and priests teach. We have not embarked upon this path casually, but with a fixed purpose and proven, thought-out means.

The Gospel and the Letters of St Paul are our guide:

a) they contain the substance of the message;
b) they mark out the mode of presentation;
c) they specify the goal: "Glory to God, peace to men";
d) they suggest the dispositions of those who write;
e) they are accompanied by God's grace;
f) they are directed to the masses first of all and then to every social class and category;
g) they are a comprehensive source of dogma, moral teaching and worship — the very things that humanity needs for eternal life.

☐   The world is evolving rapidly: population centres, culture and commerce are undergoing change. Peaceful and swift revolutions are occuring as a result of the press, televisio, radio, motion pictures, air travel, political, social and industrial stirrings, nuclear power. . . It is necessary that religion be ever present, and that everything be served of to raise the level of life on earth and attain the glory of heaven. To stop or slow down is to be overtaken, or to be relegated to a field where an adversary has already harvested.

☐ In times past (and still so in many places), soup and bread were distributed at the doors of religious houses. Today at these doors truth should be distributed. This is man's need — to know God, to know his eternal destiny.

☐ Sin is very easily multiplied. Throughout the night in every part of the world thousands of high speed presses turn out millions upon millions of copies of newspapers and magazines. Each evening, crowds of spectators are glued to picture screens. For practically the entire day, radio and television programmes are aired. . . Who is to say what percentage is healthy and what percentage harmful?

☐ A priest preaches to a meagre flock, scattered in churches that in many areas are practically empty. . . It is well for us to consider the words of Cardinal Della Costa: "Either we look at reality courageously, seeing beyond the immediate little world that surrounds us, and then grasp the urgent necessity of a radical change of mentality and method. Or, in the span of a few years, we shall have made a desert around the Master of life, and life will justly eliminate us as dead, useless and cumbersome branches".

☐ There are two dangerous deceptions:
— simply to preach against the press, radio, motion pictures and television because of the harmful content they often present. We cannot pass ourselves off as backlash critics or supporters of ignorance. We won't be heard. The Church fears only ignorance, falsehood and half-truths;
— to hold back from taking an interest in the press, radio, motion pictures and television until they are adversely organized. Preventive methods are required. It is better not to commit sin than to cry over it, better to avoid contagion than to cure sickness, better to sow good grain in a field than to allow weeds to grow. Good newspapers, good schools, worthy films, healthy television shows should have precedence. Truth first, rather than the attempt to counter error. Medicine is often inadequate and arrives too late.

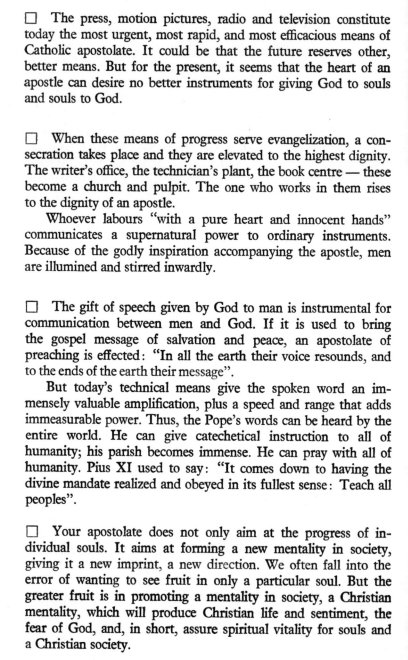

☐ The press, motion pictures, radio and television constitute today the most urgent, most rapid, and most efficacious means of Catholic apostolate. It could be that the future reserves other, better means. But for the present, it seems that the heart of an apostle can desire no better instruments for giving God to souls and souls to God.

☐ When these means of progress serve evangelization, a consecration takes place and they are elevated to the highest dignity. The writer's office, the technician's plant, the book centre — these become a church and pulpit. The one who works in them rises to the dignity of an apostle.

Whoever labours "with a pure heart and innocent hands" communicates a supernatural power to ordinary instruments. Because of the godly inspiration accompanying the apostle, men are illumined and stirred inwardly.

☐ The gift of speech given by God to man is instrumental for communication between men and God. If it is used to bring the gospel message of salvation and peace, an apostolate of preaching is effected: "In all the earth their voice resounds, and to the ends of the earth their message".

But today's technical means give the spoken word an immensely valuable amplification, plus a speed and range that adds immeasurable power. Thus, the Pope's words can be heard by the entire world. He can give catechetical instruction to all of humanity; his parish becomes immense. He can pray with all of humanity. Pius XI used to say: "It comes down to having the divine mandate realized and obeyed in its fullest sense: Teach all peoples".

☐ Your apostolate does not only aim at the progress of individual souls. It aims at forming a new mentality in society, giving it a new imprint, a new direction. We often fall into the error of wanting to see fruit in only a particular soul. But the greater fruit is in promoting a mentality in society, a Christian mentality, which will produce Christian life and sentiment, the fear of God, and, in short, assure spiritual vitality for souls and a Christian society.

☐ Let us be convinced that this apostolate calls for a greater spirit of sacrifice and a deeper piety. There will be fruitless efforts, sacrifices of sleep and time, funds that will never suffice, misunderstandings from many sides, spiritual risks of every kind, and foresight to be exercised in the choice of means. . . Save others, but first save yourself. Saints are needed to go before us on these paths, paths never before trodden and for the most part not even marked out.

This is not the stuff of amateurs, but of true apostles. Make it your business, therefore, to find the necessary light before the Tabernacle, and the grace of perseverance through the universal mediation of the Virgin Mary assumed into heaven.

☐ Our book centres are focal points of the apostolate. The open Gospel and image of St Paul indicate this. They are not commercial shops but places of service to the faithful. They do not sell but carry out an apostolate sustained by offerings. Theirs are not customers but cooperators. They are not areas of business but centres of light and warmth in Jesus Christ. Their aim is not to make money, but to serve the Church and people, not for profit but for spiritual benefit. The clergy and the people of God must find inspiration, support and direction for their ministry in them. We invite offerings rather than charge prices. The book centre mirrors our Institute. It is the point of contact between it and the people. It is the hub of distribution for all the initiatives of the Pauline apostolate. It is the publishing house of God.

The book centre is a temple. The religious who serves, a preacher. Light, holiness, joy in Jesus Christ, and Christian life are its goals. The counter is a pulpit of truth.

☐ The film apostolate is not something incidental, but of the same mission of making Jesus Christ, the Divine Master, known. It is one more means to be adopted. To circulate information, for example, one speaks, writes a letter, publishes an article, sends a telegram, uses the telephone, talks on the radio, etc., etc. Depending on circumstances, different means are put to use towards an identical end: to convey information.

And so the same zeal, the same sense of responsibility, the

K

same enthusiasm and fervent application must guide us in our work with books, films, periodicals, etc.

☐   With fervour of spirit and exaltation of heart, the greatest of the saints would attach themselves today to a microphone to launch their message of truth, justice and peace. It is impossible not to be mindful of the command of Jesus Christ: "Preach the Gospel to every creature. That which I tell you in secret, announce from the housetops". Let us reflect that it has been reserved to our times to carry out this mandate of Jesus Christ to the letter: "My word will be preached in the whole world".

17

Prayers

The following are six examples of the many prayers that Father Alberione wrote and which have become daily source of inspiration and actual forms of prayer for the members of the Pauline Family. It is easy to see in them the Founder's firm trust in God and the essence of Pauline apostolic spirituality.

The texts reproduced here are taken from the English language edition of the Manual of Prayers of the Pauline Family.

☐   A PAULINE PRAYER

O Lord, in union with all those who today celebrate the Eucharist as a memorial of Christ's death and resurrection, I offer my own self with our Lord:

— To make amends for the error spread by the misuse of the media of social communication;

— To beg your mercy for those persons who allow themselves to be led astray by the indiscriminate use of these powerful means;

— For those who knowingly reject your Son and use the media of social communication with malice;

— That all may follow him alone whom you, heavenly Father, in your boundless love gave to the world, saying: "This is my beloved Son; hear him";

— That the use of the media may help everyone learn and believe that Jesus alone is the perfect Teacher;

— That there may be a great increase in the number of priests, religious and lay persons who by prayer, example and professional work are devoted to the Christian apostolate of communications;

— That all those who work with the media of communication may strive to become holy, and proficient in their efforts, for the glory of God and the salvation of humankind;

— That we may come to know our strengths and weaknesses, and your love which alone makes us worthy to call upon you as our Father, imploring your light, compassion and mercy.

☐ PRAYER FOR THE APOSTOLATE OF SOCIAL COMMUNICATION

God our Father
to communicate your love to all
you sent into this world
your only Son, Jesus Christ.
You appointed him Master —
the Way, the Truth, and the Life —
of humankind.

Grant that the means of social communication
— press, films, radio, television —
may always be used for your glory
and for the well-being of each individual.

Raise up vocations for this manifold ministry.
Inspire men and women of good will
to contribute with prayer and work
so that through the means of social communication
the Church may preach the Good News
to the whole world.

☐ SECRET OF SUCCESS

Jesus Master, accept the pact that we present to you through the hands of Mary, Queen of the Apostles, and of our Father St Paul.

We must correspond to your sublime will, arrive at the degree of perfection and heavenly glory to which you have destined us, and carry out our apostolate in a holy manner. But we are very weak, ignorant, incapable and inadequate in every way: in spirit, in knowledge, in the apostolate and in poverty. You instead are the Way and the Truth and the Life, the Resurrection, our one and supreme Good. We trust in you alone, who said: "Whatever you ask the Father in my name, you will receive it".

For our part, we promise and commit ourselves to seeking wholeheartedly in all things, in life and in the apostolate, only and always, your glory and peace to men. We trust that on your part you will give us a good spirit, grace, knowledge, and the means for doing good. According to your immense goodness and the needs of our special vocation, multiply the fruits of our spiritual work, of our study, of our apostolate, of our poverty. We do not doubt you, but we fear our inconstancy and weakness.

Therefore, O good Master, through the intercession of Mary, our Mother, extend to us the mercy you used with the Apostle Paul so that, faithful in imitating our Father here on earth, we may be his companions in the glory in heaven.

☐ TO JESUS, THE DIVINE MASTER

Jesus, Divine Master, we adore you as the Word Incarnate sent by
the Father to instruct all men in life-giving truth. You are un-
created Truth, the only Master. You alone have words of eternal
life. We thank you for having ignited in us the light of reason and
the light of faith, and for having called us to the light of glory. We
believe, submitting our whole mind to you and to the Church; and
we condemn all that the Church condemns. Master, show us the
treasures of your wisdom, let us know the Father, make us your
true disciples. Increase our faith, so that we may attain to the
eternal vision in heaven.

☐ TO MARY, QUEEN OF THE APOSTLES

Immaculate Mary, coredemptrix of the human race, see men redeemed by the blood of your Divine Son, yet still immersed in the darkness of error and the mire of vice.

The harvest is always great, but the labourers are still very few. Have pity, O Mary, upon your children whom the dying Jesus entrusted to you from the cross. Increase religious and priestly vocations; give us new apostles full of wisdom and fervour. Sustain with your motherly care those who consecrate their lives to the good of their neighbour. Recall your care for Jesus and the Apostle John; remember your sweet petitions to the Lord to obtain the Holy Spirit for the apostles. You were the counsellor of the first apostles and of the apostles of all times. By your powerful intercession, renew again the divine Pentecost upon all those called to the apostolate; sanctify them and inflame them with holy zeal for the glory of God and the salvation of souls. Guide them in all their efforts; help them with your graces; sustain them in moments of discouragement; crown their zeal with great success. Grant our prayer, O Mary, so that all may accept the Divine Master, Way, Truth, and Life, and become docile children of the Church. May the whole world resound with your praises, and honour you as Mother, Teacher and Queen. And may we all attain eternal happiness in heaven.

Queen of Apostles : pray for us.

☐ TO ST PAUL THE APOSTLE

O Holy Apostle, who with your teaching and with your charity taught the entire world, look kindly upon us, your children and disciples.

We expect everything from your prayer to the Divine Master and to Mary, Queen of the Apostles. Grant, O Doctor of the Gentiles, that we may live by faith, save ourselves by hope, and that charity alone reign in us. Obtain for us, O Vessel of Election, docile correspondence to divine grace, so that it may not remain unfruitful in us. Grant that we may ever better know you, love you, and imitate you; that we may be living members of the Church, the mystical body of Jesus Christ. Rise up many, holy, apostles. May the warm breath of true charity permeate the entire world. Grant that all may know and glorify God and the Divine Master, Way, Truth, and Life.

The Pauline Family
in the world

Society of St Paul
Daughters of St Paul
Sister Disciples of the Divine Master
Sisters of the Good Shepherd
Sisters of the Queen of Apostles
Institute of Jesus the Priest
Institute of St Gabriel the Archangel
Institute of Our Lady of the Annunciation
Institute of the Holy Family

ARGENTINA	MALAYSIA
AUSTRALIA	MEXICO
BOLIVIA	NEW ZEALAND
BRAZIL	PAKISTAN
CANADA	PERU
CHILE	POLAND
COLOMBIA	PUERTO RICO
EL SALVADOR	SAMOA
ENGLAND	SCOTLAND
FRANCE	SPAIN
GERMANY	SWITZERLAND
HONG KONG	TAIWAN
INDIA	TANZANIA
IRELAND	UGANDA
ITALY	URUGUAY
JAPAN	U.S.A.
KENYA	VATICAN CITY
KOREA	VENEZUELA
MACAU	ZAIRE